A
COP'S
LIFE

ALSO BY SGT. RANDY SUTTON

True Blue

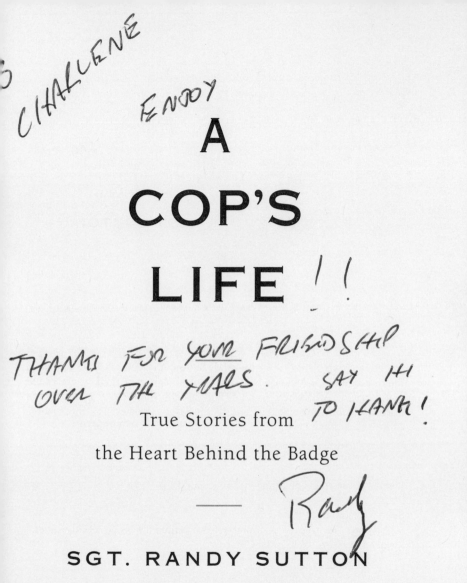

Handwritten inscription: CHARLENE ENJOY — THANKS FOR YOUR FRIENDSHIP OVER THE YEARS. SAY HI TO HANK! — Randy

A COP'S LIFE!!

True Stories from the Heart Behind the Badge

SGT. RANDY SUTTON

Edited by Cassie Wells

ST. MARTIN'S PRESS

NEW YORK

www.stmartins.com

Library of Congress Cataloging-in-Publication Data

Sutton, Randy.
    A cop's life : true stories from the heart behind the badge / Randy Sutton ; edited by Cassie Wells.—1st U.S. ed.
      p. cm.
    ISBN 0-312-33896-1
    EAN 978-0-312-33896-1
    I. Wells, Cassie. II. Title.

HV7914.S88 2005
363.2'092'273—dc 22

                                            2005042762

First Edition: July 2005

10 9 8 7 6 5 4 3 2 1

ACKNOWLEDGMENTS

THE BOOK YOU ARE ABOUT TO READ IS THE CULMINATION OF A career as a street cop. Although it is my hand that penned these stories, it is the voices of all who have worn the badge that you will hear pulsing from these pages. I am incredibly fortunate to have had the support and encouragement of a number of people of great quality who have made this book possible. My editor and friend, Cassie Wells, who lived these experiences through my words and used her great skill and compassion to guide me through and make this book a reality. "Almost Famous Author" Dan Mahoney, whose original belief in my writing led me to St. Martin's Press. George Witte and Marie Estrada of St. Martin's, who have treated me with respect and kindness throughout the entire process. My heroes and friends who have served as inspiration by their contributions to law enforcement and their friendship: Tom Michaud, Gerry Patterson, Jim Agins, Joe Pica, Vic Fassanella, Eric Cooper, Brett Shields, Scott Killabrew, Cliff Davis, Carlos Cordeiro, Dave Reid, Candy and Ray Byrd, and John Reading. Those whose friendship has been unwavering through the years: John, Pete, and Paul Soderman, Jeannie Watson, Antionette

Kuritz, Linda Cooper, Tony Matarese, and Jerry Schaefer. Cynthia Brown of *American Police Beat*, who has supported my writing from the beginning of *True Blue: Police Stories by Those Who Have Lived Them*.

Most especially, I owe my family thanks for their support and love through the years. Without it I would surely have been diminished as a human being. My mother, Lillian, and Dean, Linda, Rachel, Kristi, Martin, and Renee. And to my father, Arthur, in whose comforting shadow I shall forever walk.

Thank you.

CONTENTS

PREFACE

The Commendation

I SIT PERFECTLY STILL IN THE RECLINER, LISTENING TO THE creaking of the ice cubes as they melt into the oblivion of my scotch. Night has long given way to a dark and silent morning, and I find myself gazing at the black-framed parchment proclaiming "Cop Shows Heroism in Saving Infant's Life." How many years has this commendation been hanging on the wall in the den amid my other honors and commemorative photos illustrating, like a conscience, my nearly three decades as a cop? Ten years? Maybe more. Before tonight, I hadn't even glanced at it. *Shame*, I think. That's what I feel. And such shame cannot be reconciled with symbols of honor.

This had been my father's chair, and this had been his den. Now this is my house, but everywhere I look, especially in this room, are signs that he lived here. Over the years the soft leather had molded to his broad back, and whenever I would sink into this recliner—usually seeking insensibility in the liquor that had become my night's obsession—I would sit where he had and be enveloped in what felt like his embrace. Or was that just what I so desperately wanted to believe? As I approach the time in life when my pension is much closer than my days as a rookie cop, my own body, so similar to his, has also molded the leather, and our impressions have become indistinguishable, except that mine offers no comfort, no salvation.

He had created this wall of honors, this hall of mirrors. All these mementos of an "honorable" career had been carelessly tossed into a cardboard box and stored in my parents' garage. He had come upon them one day while sweeping the driveway. In my mind's eye I picture him on a sunny afternoon with the garage door open, shirtless, in shorts, a white cotton towel around his neck, as he spots the unmarked box shoved into a corner. Curious, he kneels down, opens it, and is surprised and pleased at what he finds. *Why,* he wonders, *isn't my son proud of what he has achieved?* He beams with pride as he lugs the box into the house to show my mother.

"Look, Lillie! Look what Randy left in the garage."

When I next came to visit he led me into the den, this den, and showed me what he had done. He had transformed an entire wall into a pictorial shrine to my accomplishments: Every commendation I had ever received was framed and accompanied by its newspaper article, invariably with a photograph of me in uniform. I was dumbstruck, chagrined, but he took my wordless response for modesty, and I can still see the kindness in his eyes as he patted my arm.

"I'm proud of you, son. So very proud of you."

Now, in these bleak hours before dawn, in this alcoholic haze, I can almost hear the laughter of the guests in the dining room down the hall, the clink of silverware against my mother's best china, the big-band–era music in the background, and then my father's wonderfully booming voice as he leads yet another group of visitors and family members into his den to show them the mementos of his youngest son. He would recount the story of each commendation, regale them with tales of my heroic deeds. The light in his eyes alone would illuminate this room and dazzle the beholders; there is no dampening of a father's love or pride. So I didn't have the courage, or the heart, to ask him to take them down. I basked in the warm glow of his respect while all the time knowing I was an impostor.

After he died and I became the sole occupant of this home, I found I couldn't take down his memorial to my heroic career. I was as haunted as this empty house. *This is the punishment I deserve,* I thought, *to sit here night after night in a maudlin stupor and feel ashamed.* Still, whatever instincts of self-preservation came into play prevented me from actually reading the inscriptions. Until tonight. Now, as I study the framed commendation across from me, the words begin to blur and a memory that I thought had been bled away over the years consumes me . . .

"Cop Shows Heroism in Saving Infant's Life"

The blistering heat of the Las Vegas summer sun made the air-conditioned patrol car barely habitable. It was a Sunday, an August afternoon, and as the mercury climbed so did the number of calls being dispatched to my sector's units. I sipped lukewarm Gatorade and waited for the next dispatch as sweat welded the back of my tan uniform to my seat. The radio's tone alert and the simultaneous buzzing of my mobile computer heralded the call that every cop prays never to hear.

"All units in Charlie area, report of an infant drowning in a pool at 1343 Riverside. Medical is being dispatched."

I immediately snatched the mike from its cradle. I was only one block from the house and could be there in seconds.

"Control, 3-Charlie-34, show me arrived."

I screeched to a stop in front of a boxy two-story house in a middle-class neighborhood. Because of the heat everyone was inside, but minivans crowded the street; this was the land of young families with small children. I threw the car in park and sprinted toward the open front door and ran through the house yelling, "Police!" not even pausing to ring the bell. I caught the turquoise glint of the backyard in-ground pool through the sliding glass door in the family room and headed that way, knocking over a dining room chair as I barreled through. As I burst from the cool temperature-controlled house into the arid backyard, it seemed as if all the sounds were suddenly muted. There was no roar of an air-conditioning unit, no radio chatter, nothing but the gentle lapping of pool water against the tile wall. What should have been a bucolic scene was perverted by what I saw before me.

A young man, not more than twenty-five, and fully dressed in jeans and a T-shirt, was wading toward the side of the pool with agonizing slowness, the water up to his neck. He was holding a limp baby in a sodden yellow romper aloft; his face had the stricken look of someone in the aftermath of a cataclysmic tornado. I knelt down and extended my arms toward him; his eyes locked on mine, and I felt his fear running like an electric current through my body and reverberating in my bones.

In those few seconds, which felt like years, I became aware of what else was happening around us. A young woman—his wife, the baby's mother—was standing beneath a brightly colored patio umbrella clutching a telephone to her chest. She was in shock, her mouth in a distorted O, and she was screaming unintelligibly and sobbing, her eyes unfocused.

"Gwwwa . . . gwwwa . . . gwwwa . . . aaaaahhh . . ."

But the young man with the infant over his head never looked at anything but me. My fingers extended out over the expanse of blue in the same way that God reaches out to Adam in Michelangelo's masterpiece on the ceiling of the Sistine Chapel, and inside I prayed, just this once, to have the same divine power over life and death. I touched her, snatched her up, and within seconds I was cradling her in one arm, breathing into her nose and mouth, giving her chest compressions with the palm of my hand. I was afraid; there was no life in her tiny form. Her skin was tinted blue, and she was very cold. The sharp smell of chlorine filled my nostrils; her downy hair was pasted to a head that barely filled the palm of my hand.

I don't know how long I stood there until the fire department paramedics came and pried the infant out of my arms. In moments they had disappeared into their ambulance, hastening to the hospital. Another officer arrived and drove the stricken parents after the ambulance. Suddenly I was completely alone in a suburban backyard, my uniform soaked with pool water, sweat, and baby's vomit. The crystalline swimming pool was still sloshing against the tiles; somewhere in the house a radio was playing a soft pop song by Barry Manilow. I could almost hear the ghostly laughter of the happy family who had been enjoying the exquisite coolness and relief of their backyard paradise until just less than an hour ago.

I sat down at the table, next to a weeping glass of iced tea, and made all the calls that duty required of me, requesting detectives, crime scene investigators, and a supervisor. I had trouble hearing dispatch over the radio: The still-rapid pounding of my heart was audible, even visible, pulsing beneath my uniform shirt, as I looked down at the impossibly small outline of the infant's body against my chest. I still tasted chlorine on my lips.

After the backyard was filled with crime scene investigators who were trying to discover the precise moment that everything went wrong, a sergeant sat down across from me. He wasn't my squad sergeant, but I had worked on the same shift with him before. He looked the part of a tough veteran cop, with his steel gray hair in a military buzz cut and an ample gut padding out his uniform. His usually affable grin was nowhere in evidence now as he leaned forward in his chair and seemed to study the pool water. I realized I hadn't moved since I sat down; my uniform was almost dry. I reached up to trace where the infant had been pressed against my chest, but all evidence of our terrible meeting had evaporated.

"I just got word from the hospital, Randy. The baby's alive."

If there is a word that can describe the overwhelming joy I felt at that moment, I can't find it. My breath caught in my throat, and I felt relief burst through the despair and uncertainty that had paralyzed me for the last hour. And I felt a flush of pride.

But the sergeant didn't smile or congratulate me. He touched my arm, his eyes sad.

"She must have been in the water too long. She has a lot of brain damage."

I wasn't ready for his words. I found myself recoiling as if I'd been shot. I had only seen life or death as the possible conclusion when I held that infant in my arms; I knew it was one or the other as I breathed into her lungs. I had never considered a third possibility. Brain damage? Neither life nor death but some hellish limbo where even hope could not prevail?

"Look, son," he said kindly, interrupting my roaring thoughts, "why don't you head home. I'll clear it."

My face was an impassive mask as I nodded and stood up. He didn't let go of my arm. I turned toward the swimming pool so that he couldn't see the tears welling up in my eyes, but I heard the huskiness in his voice as he said, "You can only try, son. That's the best any of us can do."

I just walked away without replying, unable to comprehend that, in his efforts to comfort me, he had revealed a vast reservoir of private misery inside himself. He wasn't just a veteran cop but a veteran witness to all the horrors, little and big, that police officers are subjected to. He reached out to me with compassion, with a profound understanding of what I was feeling, but I was too lost in my own misery to see it. I walked stiffly back to my sweltering patrol car, drove to the station, changed out of my uniform, and went home to an empty house where no amount of alcohol could diminish the feel of that tiny infant's cool dampness against my lips.

She lived for months, or at least that's what they called it. While her body wasted away in the antiseptic environs of the terminal ward, I was heralded for "saving a life" and given a black-framed commendation to commemorate the occasion for all eternity. When she finally died, there was no subsequent news item in the paper. "Cop Shows Heroism in Saving Infant's Life" is what everyone remembers, except, of course, for the bereft young parents. The three of us remember an entirely different conclusion to an idyllic Sunday afternoon one August.

When my father found the cardboard box full of my commendations and honors, this one particularly touched him. But I had never told him the full story. I had never talked about it at all. So he had no idea what I would feel when I walked into his den to find the story of my saving the drowning infant as the centerpiece of his collection chronicling the actions of his son, the hero.

"I'm proud of you, son. So very proud of you."

I can still see his eyes, beaming with pride, and that was not something I was willing to extinguish with the truth.

It's only later in life, well past reaching mature adulthood, that things we have done or failed to do catch up to us, even overrun us and drag us down. After my father died and his house, his den, his recliner, and the wall of honors came to me, I spent many a night sitting as I am now, sipping potent scotch by candlelight and contemplating the corrosiveness of sins of omission. And tonight, I take down the commendation my father had so proudly displayed, pry off the metal tabs that held the cardboard backing in place, and pull out the yellowed document. As I feed it to the hungry flame and watch it consumed and blackened into fragile ash, I apologize to my father for thinking me a hero, to an old sergeant who tried to comfort me, and to a little girl who I pray forgives me for failing her.

EPILOGUE. Maybe it was then, while that commendation burned, that the impetus to write down these stories was born. These are the things that I should have told my father when he was alive so that he would know me as I am—not a hero but imperfect, sometimes devastated by circumstances, sometimes paralyzed by indecision, sometimes afraid, sometimes not strong enough to bear whatever burden falls to me, sometimes self-destructive, sometimes callous and without pity, always somehow alone. I cheated him of that. My father was the man whom I admired more than anyone else, and I will be forever sorry that I never let him see me clearly and without pretense. I never gave him the opportunity to understand what my life as a cop was really like. I shielded him from something I should have shared with him. But because I know my father, I know that even if every truth contained within these pages were laid bare and bleeding in front of him, and even if they blatantly refuted the glorification implied on his wall of tribute in this silent den, he would still say:

"I'm proud of you, son. So very proud of you."

And that breaks my heart.

This book is dedicated to my father, Arthur Sutton.

A
COP'S
LIFE

JOHNNY'S LAST DAY

MY LIFE AS A COP BEGAN WITH A DEATH ON A MUDDY LOCKER room floor. As I look back on that moment now, nearly three decades later, I wonder if that tragic event was a portent of my future, if my fate, my career, had been irrevocably bound to trauma and anguish and grief. It was not an auspicious beginning but an ironic one, and now, as I trace my life in uniform back to its earliest days, as I wend my way emotionally and spiritually past so many ghosts—of cops and criminals and victims and bystanders alike—back to those earliest days, the first face I see is that of Patrolman Johnny Rogerson.

Johnny Rogerson was a crusty veteran cop approaching the magical twenty-fifth year of service, the year when the brass ring of retirement would be within his grasp. He was the desk officer at the small-town police department where I, at nineteen, was a police cadet. Like a lot of guys who became police officers after World War II, he had joined the police department straight out of the army. After more than two decades, he still had the military bearing and wore his steel gray hair in a military-style brush cut. His face was crisscrossed with deep lines, and he had the look of a rugged, albeit retired, Marlboro Man, which was fitting since he was almost never without that brand of cigarette hanging from the corner of his mouth. Johnny's job was to answer the phone, to greet citizens who stormed the desk with questions and complaints, and to dispatch officers on calls. All the patrol officers rotated between patrol and working the desk—all except Johnny. Unlike everybody else on the force, he preferred, or so I thought, to be behind the desk instead of in a patrol car. To me, he was like a giant spider in the center of its web, alert to everything and everybody who wandered into his reach, as quick to criticize as he was to console.

How did he take to me? He tended to regard me with one raised eyebrow and a lot of skepticism.

"You're too young to be here, kid," he'd say whenever I came through the door in my cadet's uniform. "What are they doing putting babies in men's boots?" he'd mutter and shake his head. "You better be fully grown before you pin a badge on your chest. Nobody's gonna hold your hand out there, boy."

So it went for most of my first year. I figured he was taunting me in a good-natured way, but I also figured that being a man, much less a police officer, involved absorbing taunts with placid indifference. Johnny Rogerson became my testing ground for handling brusque personalities. I'd respond to his jesting by smiling and shaking my head as if he'd just told a great joke. After a few weeks, I discovered we were getting along just fine.

My job, after all, was to help him at the desk. I was the only cadet in the station, a holdover from a high school internship program. When my classmates made a running leap for the wide open summer and either packed for college, left to travel through Europe on a Eurailpass, or sought a summer job that would provide gas and beer money, I put on my uniform and walked straight back to the police station. I also worked a security job during the day and took some college classes at night, but I knew, with absolute conviction, what I wanted to do with my life. It was just a matter of time.

"So what do you want to be when you grow up, boy?" Johnny would chide me as I'd sit down at my desk behind the bullet-proofed, glass-walled dispatch console that separated city hall from the police station.

"A cop," I'd say, since this had become a ritual greeting between us. "That's all I've ever wanted to be. I don't want to be anything but a cop."

"Hey," Johnny would say to a group of cops coming in from patrol. "Got some career advice for this kid? Seems he's got his heart set on being one of us."

"This job sucks!"

"Go be a banker or something."

"Go someplace where you can make some goddamned money!"

They all would laugh, and I would laugh, too, because anyone who wanted to be a cop knew it wasn't a practical choice and maybe not even a choice at all but a calling. I believed I was one of the lucky ones because I'd known what I wanted to do with my life while still in high school; becoming a cop was my sole aim. The age of majority had recently changed from twenty-one to eighteen, so it was actually possible to be a cop while still a teenager. I was intent on doing just that, even though I knew that openings didn't come up very often in a small town; usually one new recruit was hired every two years. I wasn't dissuaded; I had taken an extra load of courses in high school so that I could graduate six months early and be able to test for the department while still a cadet.

I had tested when the last opening came up a year before and had done well—just not well enough. I was number two. When the results were posted, Johnny had chuckled and clapped me on the back.

"That's just the department's way of saying, 'We like you, kid, but you're just too goddamned young.' "

The other cops were a bit more encouraging. When they passed by the front desk, they'd offer, "Hey, kid, hang in there and keep trying, you'll get somewhere."

But, God, I was frustrated. The list was only good for a year, and there wasn't going to be another cop hired until after Johnny retired, which would be after the list expired. I had tested with other departments as job announcements came out, but I really wanted to stay at my hometown department. I knew all the guys working there from the chief on down, and I felt comfortable with them. And, despite my initial reservations, I found myself looking forward to my half-shift at the desk with Johnny Rogerson.

Johnny was the "open for business" desk sergeant; he unlocked the doors to the street, ran the flag up the flagpole, made coffee, and perused the blotter, all before 6.00 A.M. No matter how early I came jogging up the steps, he would already be standing at the floor-to-ceiling window reveling in the sight of the sunrise, his GONE FISHIN' coffee mug steaming in his hand, his Marlboro cigarette at the corner of his mouth.

"Never miss a sunrise, boy," he'd say when I pushed through the double doors. "A sunrise is God's way of saying 'Praise be to Jesus, you lucky sonovabitch, you get to live another day.' " He'd smile and hand me my own mug, with ROOKIE stenciled hopefully on the side, and we'd settle down to police business.

"What the hell are you doing with slime like that?" he'd bellow to a tearful young woman who had come in to bail out the boyfriend who had slapped her around and blackened her eye. "You're better than that, missy! There's a nice young man out there who will treat you with the respect you deserve. Do yourself a favor and leave this piece of shit in jail where he belongs."

He'd listen patiently to an old lady's tearful tale of her lost cat and dispatch a patrol car to help find it. He'd lecture the twelve-year-old who had thrown water balloons off Carnegie Bridge; he'd excoriate the purse-snatcher who had dislocated a woman's arm; he'd console the elderly man whose senile wife had wandered away in Palmer Square. Whoever walked through the front door, whoever called the station, was subjected to the wisdom, advice, and judgment of desk patrolman Johnny Rogerson. It was, for me, the most entertaining show in town.

Whenever there was a lull in foot traffic and police business, Johnny would regale me with stories of his life as a cop—his life "on the road," as he called it. He told me rousing tales of foot chases and shootouts, of rescues from burning buildings, of brawls and barricaded hostage incidents. Whenever he told me of a particularly harrowing caper, he would get a faraway look in his eyes as if he were reliving his time as a young cop on the street and savoring the memory. Whenever he told me about a particularly tragic call, his eyes would fill with tears and his voice would fade to a whisper. Dead babies, injured children, fallen officers—I was nearly moved to tears, too. *This is what it will be like,* I thought, and I was captivated by the idea of such an amazing, adventurous life. I would listen, mesmerized, and then later, when I was alone, I would project myself into his stories and become the valiant hero cop. I'd be Johnny or I'd be his partner, and his adventures and experiences became the objects of my envy. I even told him that once.

"Nothing to envy, son. You'll have your own 'adventures' one day—God help you." He'd smiled. I was coming to learn that behind that gruff exterior there was a gentle and uncomplicated man. In my head, I'd always known I wanted to be a cop, but listening to Johnny Rogerson made my dream a desire from the heart.

I was sitting in the study lounge of my college campus one day, so lost in the fantasy that I, too, was a veteran cop and that Johnny Rogerson and I were trading war stories like a pair of battle-weary warriors, that I missed the bell for class. *Envy again,* I thought. *Or maybe simple admiration.* I wondered if he had ever thought to write his memoirs, to write down his amazing stories. Since I had missed my class anyway, I went into the campus bookstore and bought one of those soft-cover notebooks with the black-and-white pebbly design. The next morning I brought it to him. He took a long drag on his cigarette and looked at it with squinty eyes.

"There's an idea, kid. There's an idea," he said, and he thanked me with an odd smile on his face. As he dropped the notebook in the bottom drawer of his desk, I wondered if I had offended him somehow.

One day when we were logging reports I thought to ask the obvious.

"Hey, Johnny, why'd you come inside anyway? You could still be out working the streets, right? You could rotate from the front desk to patrol if you wanted, couldn't you?"

He looked up at me, cocked an eyebrow, and grinned. "Come with me," he said.

I followed him back into the locker room, where he opened his gun locker and showed me a big calendar with all the days until his retirement listed and numbered in countdown form. Big red X's marked the days that had passed. He pulled out a small metal box and opened it up for me to see. It was chock-full of bro-chures and photographs cut out from magazines: deep sea fishing off the coast of Baja California; trout fishing in the Pacific North-west; an Alaskan cruise; mountain cabins for sale in the Ozarks; bus tours of New England; dude ranches in Montana; even paragliding in Venezuela. There were also pictures and cards from his two grandchildren in Arizona enjoining him to come for a visit.

"Two hundred and sixty-one days, kid, and the world is my oyster. It's just a matter of deciding what to do first."

I don't know where it came from, but I felt anger flooding through my gut. All I wanted was to get on the force; all he wanted, apparently, was to leave it. He knew how badly I wanted this job. He'd put in his full twenty-five; it would cost him noth-ing to move up his retirement date so that I would be eligible to take his place.

But my irrational anger quickly dissipated in the face of his unabashed joy. My future was not dependent on what Johnny did, and I knew that and so found myself taking pleasure in hear-ing about his ever-changing future plans in much the same way I'd enjoyed his never-ending war stories.

"Two hundred and forty days, kid," he'd say as I set his coffee mug in front of him on the desk: black with two sugars, just the way he liked it.

At 180 days, he starting taking the calendar out of his locker each morning and bringing it up to the desk, where we could both contemplate those rows of red X's. *Maybe that's what a life consists of,* I thought idly, *an endless series of days that have been simply and succinctly eliminated.* I was very young then and didn't yet feel the bitter nostalgia that is too often tethered to the pas-sage of time.

It was late fall when I found myself sitting next to Patrolman Robert Simms in the anteroom outside the chief's office. I had an appointment with the chief to see if I could retain my list status at number one rather than retest, even though I knew that rollover was not allowed. If I slipped to number two again, I would end up waiting another year or more. I thought it wouldn't hurt to ask. Simms was in there to talk about vacation time. He studied the toes of his polished boots while I studied the ceiling.

"How do you like old Rogerson?" he asked me.

"He took some getting used to," I said, and he laughed.

"Yeah, but if you get the old bastard on your side, you've got a friend for life. And you won't find a better friend or a better cop anywhere."

"You worked with Rogerson on the street?"

"Six years—hell of a street cop."

"Everybody says that," I acknowledged. "Makes me wonder why he hung it up."

Simms turned to me. "Wasn't his choice. He didn't tell you? Johnny had a heart attack a couple of years ago. A mild one, sure, but the chief pulled him inside and made him permanent desk man. You've gotta be young and healthy to work the streets."

I was dumbfounded—I had never thought of Johnny as anything but robust. The rigors of the street would be nothing to him, I'd believed. I wondered why he hadn't told me; I couldn't imagine any two cops working closer together than we had those last months. It dawned on me that though I wasn't even a rookie yet, he was my partner.

As I walked into the police station the next morning, Johnny was standing at the floor-to-ceiling window watching the sunrise with his usual rapt appreciation through the tendrils of smoke from his ever-present Marlboro cigarette. It was the sixth day on

Johnny's seven-day shift—in those days cops worked seven days in a row before getting a couple of days off—and for the first time I noticed that he looked tired. The skin beneath his eyes was puffy, almost bruised looking, but he greeted me with a wide grin.

"Gonna rain like a sonovabitch tomorrow, kid."

I looked at the rosy pink horizon, and I'll be damned if I saw anything other than the start of a brilliant autumn day. "Not a chance, Johnny. You've been looking at the wrong page in the *Farmers' Almanac.*"

"Nope," he said. "It's gonna rain."

When I came back from getting our coffees, I found him standing in front of his days-to-retirement calendar with his red marker in his hand.

"My time's approaching," he said as he took his GONE FISHIN' mug from my hands. We both stood there staring at the most recent *X*. In an odd bit of fanciful thinking, I realized that the *X* bore the shape of an hourglass, and it almost seemed as if I could actually see the minute granules of sand slipping through that pinched portal where the two lines met.

"Son," he said softly, and I turned to look at him. He'd never called me anything but "kid" or "boy" before, so it took me by surprise. "It's too bad that stupid list expires before I go. There's nobody I'd rather see take my spot than you. You're going to make a good cop someday."

As he walked past me, he brushed his hand along my shoulder. I remember being deeply touched by that simple gesture and by what he had said. I also remember feeling a sharp pang of guilt for having wished that his retirement date would come up before the list expired.

The rest of the morning was quiet and uneventful. When it was time for me to head to my security job, I just waved to

Johnny as I stepped outside; if I remember correctly, he was on the phone with a frantic mother whose nine-year-old son had accidentally dropped his iguana in the toilet.

By late afternoon the clouds had started to roll in, and the State Emergency Bureau began issuing storm warnings. By early evening it had started raining pretty hard, and the forecast was saying that a severe tropical storm, even a hurricane, was headed our way. *Johnny called it*, I acknowledged, grinning to myself. I wasn't too concerned with the dire forecast; we hadn't seen hard weather in a very long time, so I thought it was just typical weatherman's hype.

The next morning, however, I awoke to the sounds of a howling wind and a driving rain battering my bedroom window. I looked out into the gray deluge and saw the wind whipping the trees, even snapping the trunks of the saplings planted last spring, and saw torrents of water rushing down the street, making parked cars look as if they were lodged in the middle of a fast-moving river. I turned on the TV and saw that the storm was about to be reclassified as a hurricane. The mayor was calling for everybody who could stay home and wait the storm out to do so.

It was my one day off during the whole week, but I knew they would need help down at the police station, so that's where I wanted to be. The short drive was surreal: Uprooted vegetation littered the sidewalk, and the road was aswirl in mud. As I drove along at ten mph, hurtling tree branches slammed into my windshield and pounded into the roof of my car. I got completely soaked as I ran from my car up the steps to the police station, so I stood just in front of the double doors to shake myself off. That's how I happened to be looking out toward the horizon much as Johnny did every day to watch the sunrise. This time there was no rosy hue of a burgeoning dawn: The horizon was matte black and ominous with tendrils of threatening gunmetal gray clouds swirling upward. *It looks,* I thought, *like the end of the world.*

Inside, it was controlled pandemonium.

"I'm glad you're here," the sergeant said as I walked through the door. "Take the desk. We're swamped."

"Where's Johnny?" I asked, surprised that he wasn't sitting in his usual place.

"Didn't make it in. Hell, look at what's happening out there. I'm surprised you even made it through that shit."

I wasn't wearing my uniform, but I didn't bother going to the locker room to change; I sat down and started answering the phones. Patrolman Dave Johnson came in, and together we dispatched the patrol cars. For the next few hours we witnessed the storm growing in intensity and the call volume swell in proportion to the floodwaters. It was nerve-racking, and neither of us moved from our places at the console for the entire morning.

Finally, toward 3:00 P.M., as it was nearing the time for the shift to change, there was a lull in the storm and, unbelievably, a lull in the incoming calls. I knew I wasn't going anywhere until the storm had completely abated, so while Dave made coffee I ran downstairs to the locker room to splash cold water on my face and to change into my uniform.

I went charging through the locker room door, slipping and nearly falling in the mud that had been tracked in by the officers working the night shift. As I veered around the corner toward my locker, I felt the breath catch in my throat: There was a body lying on its side next to the wooden bench separating the rows of lockers. Its shirt was the familiar midnight blue color of the department's uniform. I stepped forward like a sleepwalker, not sure on this most unreal of days whether I was imagining it. As I knelt down I saw that it was Johnny.

He was curled up in an almost fetal position with his face turned toward the wall of lockers, his hands balled into fists against his chest. I pulled him over on his back and saw that his half-opened eyes were rheumy and staring. His face was ashen, and vomit leaked out of the corner of his mouth and down the front of his uniform shirt. What I didn't comprehend then, but I remember vividly now, was that he was ice cold to the touch, his limbs stiff and his lips blue. I had never seen death before; I didn't know where hope receded and finality began.

"Help me! Help me!" I screamed up the stairs. "Johnny's had a heart attack! Call the rescue squad!"

My training kicked in. I pulled his rigid body into a more open area on the muddy locker room floor and reached in between his teeth with my fingers to clear out the vomit. Then I began mouth-to-mouth resuscitation simultaneously with chest compressions.

"One one thousand . . . two one thousand . . . three one thousand . . . Somebody help me!"

His lips felt like frozen ribs of ice against mine, but when I felt his chest swell slightly with my exhalations I kept at it.

Then the locker room was filled with cops. Uniformed legs surrounded me, but no one knelt down to help.

"Take over!" I screamed, wanting someone to continue the chest compressions while I concentrated on filling his lungs with air. There was only silence.

I felt hands pulling me up, pulling me away from Johnny, and I found myself looking into the sergeant's kindly face.

"Randy, Johnny's dead. There's nothing you can do for him, son. Look at him. Go on."

And I did; I looked down at that still and pitiful form on the muddy floor, and I knew it was true. He had been dead for hours, probably since he'd come into the station early that morning. My legs seemed to give out under me, and I found myself sitting on the locker room bench while the other cops made way for the rescue squad. While they loaded up his body and took it away, I just listened to all the voices around me.

"Jesus Christ! Right in the fucking police station!"

"Didn't anybody think to look for him?"

"This isn't fucking fair."

"Who's going to call his family?"

"Will somebody answer that goddamned phone?!"

"Randy? Randy, are you all right?"

"Yeah," I said. "Just give me a minute."

I stumbled into the bathroom and bolted the door. For the next twenty minutes I rinsed my mouth out with cold water, trying to get rid of the taste of death and decay. I rubbed at my lips so hard with my thumb that I made them bleed. Yet I could still taste it. I looked at myself in the mirror, and for a moment I saw Johnny's image, his face ashen, his lips blue. I closed my eyes, took a ragged breath, swallowed the bile that was rising in the back of my throat, and opened the door into the locker room.

It was empty. Johnny's body was gone, and so were all the other cops. Where he'd been lying on the floor there was just a muddy smear. I stood motionless for a moment, looking down, and then realized Johnny's locker was ajar. *He must have just opened it when he was stricken,* I thought.

I found an empty box in the trash, and for the next half hour I carefully emptied out his locker. I wrapped his GONE FISHIN' mug in newspaper, stacked his travel destination brochures and pictures, folded up his street clothes, collected his Marlboro cigarettes, and took down the photographs of his two grandchildren from where they were taped to the inside of his locker door. I wanted to make sure his family got these things, that they weren't forgotten or merely discarded. For a long time I looked at the calendar with the big red *X*'s until, almost without realizing what I was doing, I crumpled it up and flung it in the trash can. I was about to shut the locker when I noticed something that had been shoved to the back of the top shelf: It was the pebbly black-and-white notebook I'd given Johnny the summer before.

I opened it and saw his familiar handwriting at the top of the first page. In red ink he'd written "A Cop's Life." That was all he'd written; there was nothing else.

I set the box of Johnny's belongings next to the console at the front desk and told the sergeant that I was going home.

"You did everything you could, Randy," he said to me. "It was just his time."

I nodded dumbly and walked toward the double doors, that bad taste of death and vomit still burning in my mouth.

Patrolman Simms was standing in front of the station smoking a cigarette while watching the afternoon sun valiantly attempt to break through the residue of the storm. When he saw me he nodded, an acknowledgment of our shared loss, of futility, of life just going on, all in that single simple gesture. I stood beside him, watching the clouds, and we didn't say anything for a long time. Then he turned to me and grinned.

"I guess congratulations are in order, kid."

"What?" I said, confused.

"You're going to be one of us now, aren't you?"

Yes, I suddenly realized, *I am.*

SUNDAY MOURNING

PATROL. PUSHING A BLACK-AND-WHITE. WORKING THE STREETS. Different ways to describe the same job: being a cop. It's what I do and what I've done for more than twenty-five years. The job isn't who I am but what I've experienced. The visions and the sensations cannot help having colored my world. As any cop knows, humor, cruelty, and stupidity are served up on a daily basis, and the calls, the years, the faces blur together like some inner-city mural that aristically evokes the essence of a neighborhood nobody really stops to look at anymore. But as the years pass, I find there are solitary moments that stand out, that I don't lose sight of. That I can't lose sight of.

A spring morning with a cobalt blue sky and just enough of a clean, fresh breeze to make me want to breathe in deep and absorb the pungent scents. The tranquility of a quiet Sunday. The suburban landscape revealed budding trees, freshly mown lawns, and dutiful husbands doing yard work under the approving gaze of their wives.

I was headed nowhere in particular when I heard the screaming of a car's tires and the explosion of metal and glass on impact. It was just ahead, in the next intersection: a small orange car had smashed headfirst into a telephone pole. My adrenaline surged as I hit the gas and grabbed the handheld mike from its berth next to my radio and gave my location to dispatch. I asked them to roll medical in case there were injuries, and within moments I had pulled up to the scene of the accident.

The first thing I noticed was that a small plume of smoke was rising up from the hood of the car where the front end was crumpled against the pole. Maybe that was to be expected, but I felt a clenching in my gut when I saw the smoke, or smelled it—both senses alerted me to the danger. I radioed a request to the fire department, jumped out of my patrol car, and ran over to the wreck.

In just the few moments that it took me to reach the car, the smoke had begun thickening, darkening. An acrid stench assaulted my lungs. As I grabbed hold of the driver's door handle I saw a young man pinned behind the steering wheel. He looked up at me, meeting my eyes, and I saw blood coursing down his face from a gash on his forehead. His brown hair was matted with sweat and blood as he tried to push open his door from the inside. I was pulling, he was pushing, our hands only inches apart yet separated by almost solid metal. The door had wedged shut from the impact.

His panicked eyes held mine as he tried to yell through the glass, but I read his lips more than I heard him.

"Help me! I can't get out! Help me, please, please!"

I sprinted over to the passenger's side and jerked on the door, but that, too, was wedged shut. The smoke was now billowing out from under the car and starting to pour into the passenger compartment.

"I'll get you out!" I shouted as I ran back to the patrol car to grab the nightstick in the driver's door.

The young man's face was pressed against the window and his bloody hand was beating impotently against the glass as I ran back to him. I could hear him screaming even as his face disappeared in the churning smoke. I had raised the nightstick, determined to break out the window in a single blow, when the passenger compartment exploded into flame, searing my face, singeing off my eyebrows and some of my hair, the impact throwing me backward and onto the asphalt.

I struggled to my feet; the heat was so intense that I couldn't get within ten feet of the car. I could only stand there, helpless and numb, and watch him burn to death. His final scream was so tortured that it became like a living thing, disconnected from time and place and even from the young man himself, and I still hear it clearly to this day.

It seemed like an eternity, but it was only a few minutes until the fire department arrived. All that was left after their ministrations was a smoldering wreck, the young man indistinguishable from the charred metal that had become his pyre. A crowd had gathered, but it was very quiet; I could hear the water dripping from the car's undercarriage, the hiss of steam, the firemen's boots scraping against the asphalt. Then a young woman pushed through the crowd and made her way over to me. She was trembling with anger, with disgust.

"Why didn't you do something?"

I gazed beyond her trying to formulate a reply. His final scream made all excuses moot. The answer didn't come. It never has, it never will.

405

IT WAS THAT NETHER HOUR, A GRAVEYARD-SHIFT COP'S NO-man's-land, when the night's over but dawn has yet to set the horizon aglow, when dispatch sent me a message over my mobile computer. My patrol car seemed to be gliding through the deserted housing-project streets, lulling me into a state of near insensibility, but I stirred from my lethargy long enough to hit the acknowledge button so that the dispatcher would know I'd received it. I wondered idly if she was as tired as I was. My eyes burned with fatigue as they played over the text.

"Sergeant," it read, "you might want to be aware of 1S34's call. It's event 1246."

"Jesus Christ," I muttered to myself. I hated graveyard, and all the hostility I felt at being assigned to this shift now included both the inanimate machine resting on my console and whatever citizen had the audacity to report an emergency at this ridiculous hour of the morning. My anger served to wake me up, and I stabbed at the buttons that would bring up the details of event 1246. 1S34 was a rookie cop with less than six months street time. He'd been assigned to graveyard, as are all rookies on the

Las Vegas PD, in order to get the requisite seasoning: bad hours, hot calls, drunks, druggies, strippers, and desperate gamblers hoping for one big score mixed in a soup of never-ending neon. This was the land of "war stories," where every freshman patrol-officer accumulates enough anecdotes, embellished with each retelling, to last him his entire career. With more than twenty years on the job, I was fresh out of novel experiences and was just hoping to get through another night unscathed, but I was the sergeant in charge. This rookie was my responsibility and, like it or not, I had to "guide" him through his street initiation.

"Control, 614. Copy that."

I dropped the radio back in its cradle and turned to read the screen's glowing green digital message. The address was one of the new apartment complexes that are being vomited up all over Las Vegas to create barely-living space for the thousands of hope-fuls who move there monthly to chase the desert pot o' gold. That pot shows up about as frequently as the one at the end of the proverbial rainbow, but that's never dissuaded the émigrés-from-anywhere from their futile quest.

I have a certain wary respect for the words on the patrol car's computer console screen: Too often what's written there is a harbinger of doom, the first indication that someone's life is about to be altered forever. Officer Ryan, aka 1S34, was to "see the reporting woman," who had awoken to find her husband missing and a suicide note left behind on the bedside table. *Let's hope,* I mused, *that this is just a cry for help and not a true 405,* the code for a suicide. It's been my experience that such notes or phone messages are delivered when there is an ex or soon-to-be-ex in the picture and the distraught or jilted spouse needs some attention or pity or forgiveness. Sometimes such a note works; sometimes it doesn't. I read the description of the missing man; he was twenty-four years old, white-blond hair in a crew cut, blue eyes, six-four with a slim build. As with most of these calls, his description made him sound as if he had plenty to live for.

I sat up a little straighter when I became aware of how deeply in my seat I was slouching. This call had the "feel of real" to me, so I reached again for my portable mike.

"Control, 614. I'll be en route to 1-Sam-34's call."

I could have just punched the message directly to dispatch via the computer, but by going live over the air I was letting both Officer Ryan and the other patrol units out there know that I was taking this call seriously and I wanted them to do the same. This way, too, all units without a call pending would head up to the area to assist without being asked.

I was still on my way as I heard, over radio traffic, Ryan arriving at the apartment. The sky had changed, and I could see that the sun was about to make its regal entrance over the distant Sunrise Mountain. For a moment I felt a sense of exhilaration. The shift would be over soon, and I would be free to do as I pleased by the light of what looked like it would be a beautiful day. Then the tone alert signifying an emergency pierced the lulling chatter on the radio.

"All units, report of a man down on West Sahara near Durango. Reported by a cellular phone."

I had a sinking feeling in my gut. The call was one block from the apartment of the missing man, three blocks from where I was now. It was an area where the land was just being leveled for new construction. I would be the first on the scene, and I already knew what I would find there. I was sure that Ryan had heard it over his portable radio; I just hoped that the wife had not.

"All units responding on the man down, only additional is that he is lying on the grass on the south side of the street and reportedly there is a shotgun near him."

Oh, shit, I thought. The gut feeling was turning into a certainty.

"Control, 614 has arrived the area."

I slowed down my patrol car so that I could search the terrain visually. There was a newly laid concrete sidewalk with grassy areas on both sides. One grassy area abutted the street; the other extended toward the rocky undeveloped desert. The little pink surveyor flags flapping gaily in the early morning breeze struck me as absurdly festive. It took me a few moments to find it, but there it was—a body sprawled atop the sod separating the sidewalk from the desert, as if gunned down while trying to make a break for the wide open space.

I pulled my squad car to the curb on the wrong side of the road and activated my overheads so that the inevitable parade of investigators, crime scene specialists, and coroner technicians that shows up at the final act of violent death would be able to find the scene. On the off chance that the "body" was not a body yet but a victim clinging to life, I jumped out of my patrol car and trotted over.

The automated sprinkler system had activated all along the grassy strip, and everything, including the blond crew-cut corpse, was dappled with moisture. He was lying face up, and I didn't need to check his pulse to see that death had already pounced. The eyes always tell you: hooded and dull, staring unfocused at nothing. In life, his eyes must have been a brilliant blue, a vivid Adriatic blue, but now they were muddy gray, the hopeless color of storm-drain runoff. I knelt beside him anyway, more like a mourner than a cop, and allowed myself a few seconds of respectful silence. Those first few moments alone with a person taken by violent death are macabrely intimate and not something you ever get used to.

"614, advise if medical is needed." The dispatcher's voice startled me to my feet. My tired eyes scanned the rest of the body. The single-barreled shotgun lay across his legs at an angle. Judging by the deep red gore bubbling from the hole in the front of his sodden khaki-colored shirt, he had placed the barrel directly against his chest and over his heart. I didn't have to turn him over to know that there was a huge exit wound in his back. The blood that had drained out of him was soaking into the moisture-rich grass and sod and mixing with the water from the sprinklers. The unnatural paleness of his face combined with the beads of water clinging to his skin made him look as if he'd just broken a high fever. That, along with the flapping pink flags and the burgeoning dawn, made the scene seem oddly peaceful.

"Control, 614. Negative on the medical. Roll detectives and criminalistics and advise the watch commander. I need two units to assist at the scene, and have 1S34 call me on my cell phone," I radioed.

I turned away from the body and toward the mountains, where the rising sun was silhouetting the peaks like an inky watercolor painting. I pretended for a moment that I was up there in the pine forest, seated next to a campfire, warming my hands around a coffee mug. I hated looking at corpses, especially suicides. The utter finality of this young man's decision filled me with a hopeless sense of frustration bordering on rage.

"Fucking idiot," I said aloud to this boy at my feet, who would never see another sunrise, much less this one, which was perhaps the most glorious I'd ever seen. The cell phone hanging on my gun belt shrilled into my consciousness as I watched two black-and-whites driving up the empty road toward me.

"Sergeant Sutton."

"Sarge, it's Ryan."

"You hear my radio traffic?" I asked.

"Yeah. It's him, huh?"

"That'd be my guess," I told him. "Physical description matches."

In the background I could hear a woman sobbing, and I winced inwardly at what I had to ask Ryan to do.

"He used a shotgun. I need for you to confirm with the wife that he had one, okay?" I hesitated for a moment as I glanced down at the young man's pale face. "What's his name?"

"David. According to the wife he just turned twenty-four last week."

Then he spoke softly, as if he had turned out of earshot.

"That's the same age as me, Sarge."

The odd way he said this struck me like a fist in the gut, but I had to stay focused on business.

"Does she have any idea why?"

"She said he'd been upset over money issues. He'd gotten a couple of nasty phone calls from his ex-wife about back support payments, and yesterday he got a subpoena for a civil suit."

Ah, I thought, *I knew there was an ex in the equation somewhere.*

"Ryan, what did the note say?"

"He just apologized, Sarge. Said he was sorry he couldn't do better like he had promised her. Sarge?" He was almost whispering into the phone. "They've only been married for two months."

This had nothing to do with the investigation; it was one young man's way of trying to find out why another young man would take his own life. Both these young men had just started to live, and now one was lying dead at my feet and the other was whispering his dread into my ear. I wished I had something soothing to tell the rookie, but in more than twenty years I'd never found the answers myself.

"Ryan, we can never understand some things. We can never know why for someone the pain inside is so bad that . . ." *That what?* I thought. *That there is no hope, not for a future, not for the buoyancy of love, not for overcoming all the little obstacles that make our paths so arduous, not for another astounding sunrise?*

"Sarge?"

"Is there someone you can call for his wife, Ryan? Any family?" No one should be alone when tragedy drops like a leaded shroud.

"His father," Ryan told me. "She called him when she found the note, and now he's on his way over here."

"Okay. Stay with her until he arrives and the detectives get there."

I pushed the end-call button and returned the cell phone to its perch on my gun belt, then turned my attention to the two young patrolmen who were busy stringing yellow crime scene tape, using their black-and-whites to mark off an area big enough to satisfy the detectives and the crime scene personnel. A suicide is treated as a homicide until the dicks wave their magic investigative wands and declare it otherwise. I was thinking that I would rather be here than where Ryan was; it was emotionally safer than the contagion of grief he was facing now.

I was about to send one of the guys on a coffee run, because I figured we'd be there awhile, when I saw a blue compact coming slowly up the deserted road toward us. Since the road didn't lead anywhere, there shouldn't have been any through traffic, so I kept an eye on the car's approach. Rubberneckers at a crime scene are as common as maggots on a decomposing body, so when the car slowed, I wasn't surprised. He was a heavyset, gray-haired man, midfifties maybe, with his neck craned, looking with dumb fascination at the yellow crime scene tape. I was leaning against my patrol car's fender, and as he passed by me, I was about to tell him through his open car window to keep his eyes on the road. Suddenly he became aware of me and turned toward me, stopping his car, his eyes wide and confused, and I knew who he was. His eyes were that same brilliant color, that vivid Adriatic blue. From where we were the body wasn't completely visible; all that could be seen was the soles of the young man's work boots. The older man tore his eyes from mine. I watched him as he looked over to where the body was, then looked away and stared straight ahead, gripping the steering wheel in the same way I'd seen drunks do when they were too intoxicated to drive.

He sat like that for nearly a full minute, and I didn't have the heart to break his concentration; he was teetering emotionally at the brink, but from there it's still possible to deny what is happening. Then I saw that he was shuddering, almost convulsing, so I pushed myself away from my patrol car and leaned into his window. I was close enough to see the gray wisps of hair lift from his thinning pate in the breeze; I could see his chest rise and fall with ragged breaths. He turned and faced me, and I felt those unbelievably blue eyes lock onto mine, forging some irrevocable connection.

"It's him, isn't it?" The words were soft, almost reverent.

I felt the heat rise into my face. I knew that the next words, once spoken, were irretrievable and would forever play over and over in his mind, and in mine.

"It is. I'm sorry." The words sounded so hollow and inappropriate that I wished they'd come from someone else's lips. He nodded simply and dropped his chin, clamping his eyes shut so that tears immediately began to run down his cheeks until they dropped off the gray stubble on his fleshy chin. He pressed his lips together so tightly that they blanched, but still they could not contain the anguished moan that erupted. His car door flew open. He stumbled as he forced his bulky frame out of the compact, and I knew he was going to make a run for the body. I jumped in front of him and grabbed hold of his shoulders just as I heard the urgent footfalls of the two cops, thinking I was in trouble, running toward us.

"It's okay! It's okay!" I yelled. "I've got this!"

I turned to the man. I could feel him deflating in my grip. His blue eyes were mutely beseeching, pleading.

"No," I said softly. "You don't want to see him like this."

He trembled for a moment, then collapsed against me, his body racked by gut-wrenching sobs. I put my arms around him and watched as the sun crested the shadowed mountains as it always did, oblivious to whatever human chaos or suffering lay below. I thought how terribly sad this was, this man who had just suffered an inconsolable loss, blindly reaching out to someone to comfort him and finding only a cop he didn't know to keep him from falling headfirst into the abyss. I felt ashamed of my own inadequacy and my earlier pettiness.

I heard the sprinklers click off, inhaled the rich odor of the new grass and damp earth, and heard him muttering over and over again, "A father should not bury his son . . . A father should not bury his son . . . A father should not bury his son . . ."

Or maybe it was my own voice I heard. I just don't know.

GRAVEYARD

THE MARCH NIGHT BELONGED TO THE DESERT WIND. IT SENT waves of bitter cold washing through the Las Vegas valley with such velocity that our patrol car actually rocked as we cruised slowly down the almost deserted streets.

It was 3:00 A.M., and my new partner, Glen, was less than enthusiastic about being assigned to the relentless nights of the graveyard shift. He was hunkered down in the passenger seat, his hands thrust into his PD jacket, the collar pulled up over his red-tipped ears.

"I hate the fucking cold," he burst out. "I moved away from Chicago to get away from the fucking cold."

"Time to invest in some thermals," I replied cheerily. "This is what it's like out here at this time of the year."

"Yeah," he muttered. "Graveyard shift in this fucking ghetto."

We were assigned a beat that was far from the neon glow of the Strip, far from the glamour that Las Vegas is famous for. The cash that the average tourist threw away on the thirsty green felt was a week's salary for those in this neighborhood lucky enough to have a job. For many of the people who populated our beat, any cash that happened their way would be quickly spent on rock cocaine and cheap wine. The dopers and the drunks would huddle in Housing Authority doorways shooting dice and selling crack with a watchful eye on the empty streets, on the lookout for the bad-for-business black-and-whites that might represent an unscheduled trip to the county jail. "Five-oh!" would echo through the housing project within seconds of the patrol car turning onto the streets "claimed" by various gangs. The gangbanger sentries would stare sullenly at us as we slid past, their pistols and sawed-offs hidden in nearby bushes or deep in jacket pockets.

I'd been riding this beat for four years, and although I had the seniority to bump to days or swing, I liked working these streets during the dark time. Action was my drug of choice, and hot calls were common in the late evening and early morning hours. Things did tend to slow up around 3:00 A.M., and tonight the cold had helped to keep things pretty quiet. Our dispatcher's cool monotone would soon change that.

"Control, 1-Charlie-34. Report of a possible domestic violence in progress. A man beating a woman at 836 Weller Court, apartment 2B."

My partner was not overly impressed or concerned. He reluctantly pulled his hands out of his jacket pockets and reached for the mike we'd left dangling on the rearview mirror.

"Control, 1-Charlie-34. We copy and are en route, ETA 2."

He tossed the mike back onto its perch, glaring at it as if it were personally responsible for his misery, and then slouched back into his seat mumbling epithets as I piloted the patrol car the few blocks to the call.

This particular housing complex had been built in the 1970s, and it covered a full city block. It consisted of squat, two-story cinder-block buildings, each with four cramped apartments.

Welfare families trying to get by on meager government subsidies populated it. Streetlights, used by gangbangers for target practice, had a very short life span, so the entire complex was shrouded in darkness. Broken bottle fragments crunched beneath our combat boots as we left the warmth of our unit and walked side by side to the door of 2B. The gusty wind kept the few people visible on the street bunched in sheltering alcoves, but eyes followed our every move. The darkness was a tactical advantage for the gang-bangers, but we were, by necessity, habitués of the night, too.

As we walked up to the door of 2B, both of us noticed that it was ajar. Simultaneously we drew our service pistols and moved to opposite sides of the door. "Ambush" flashed through my mind, and the look in Glen's eyes told me that he'd thought the same thing. Then we heard a piercing scream come from the bow-els of the apartment. I pushed the door open with my boot. It was completely dark inside, and I felt the adrenaline pumping through my system. Glen nodded at me, and I whispered into the portable radio.

"Control, 1-Charlie-34. Officer entering."

I went in low to the left as Glen went to the right, both of us sweeping the room with our pistols. The screaming had come from upstairs, but we needed to clear the first floor to make sure nothing was going to take us by surprise. As we moved slowly and silently through the pitch-black apartment, we used our flashlights to illuminate the kitchen, the dining room, the living room. In the hallway we came upon a closed closet door, and Glen grasped the doorknob, waiting for my signal to open it. I gave him a quick nod when I was in position: my .45 in my right hand and pointed at the door, my flashlight turned off but at the ready in my left hand. Glen jerked the door open at the moment I switched on my light, and the sight of a thin, gray-haired old man holding a butcher knife in front of his chest nearly gave me a heart attack. Glen, who couldn't see him from his position, dropped to a combat crouch when he heard me croak, "Drop it!" as I squeezed down on the trigger. The knife instantly clattered to the floor as the old man threw his skinny arms up in the air.

"Don't shoot me! Please don't shoot me!"

"What the hell are you doing in the closet?!" The shock of almost shooting this guy was evident in my voice.

"I had to be in here. There's a crazy muthafucka upstairs."

This revelation was punctuated by another scream from upstairs and the thumping sound of a struggle.

"Get the hell out of here," I told him, and the old man scampered out of the closet, out the door, and into the night. Without a pause, Glen and I headed up the stairs. At the top we saw light coming out from under a closed door, and from behind it we heard the familiar slapping sound of a beating in progress. Then we heard another scream. This time we could identify it as female. We also heard a male voice.

"I'm gonna kill you, bitch!"

I kicked open the door. We were met with a blast of heat and the stench of sweat and fear and the sight of a shirtless man in blue jeans yanking a tiny woman close to him by her torn shirt. She was bleeding badly from her nose and from a cut by her eye, which was swollen almost shut. His arm was cocked back to punch her again when I yelled, "Freeze!"

He paused long enough to turn his head in my direction, but in less time than it took me to lunge the few steps to grab him, he pushed the woman away and turned and dove through the window, arms outstretched like Superman taking flight. The sound of his body crashing through the glass reverberated like a gunshot in the stuffy room.

"Holy shit!" Glen yelled as we both charged for the stairs. The shirtless man was picking himself up amid the broken glass, and he turned to face us as we ran into the courtyard. I was so amazed that he could even be standing after diving out of a second-story window that I hesitated, and he took the opportunity to launch himself at me full force, roaring as he came, his bare torso now slick with sweat and blood. I grabbed him around his chest as we both went down onto the splotchy grass and littered dirt. I could smell the sour wine on his breath and see the rage in his eyes; I latched my hands behind him, pinning his arms at his sides, trying to keep him from raising his fists. Then he went totally limp and began twitching spasmodically. His eyes rolled back in his head. I released my grip and rolled out from under him, moving away on all fours like a skittering crab. I looked up at Glen, who was standing with an expression of disbelief on his face.

"Call for medical!" I yelled, and he yanked his portable radio from his belt and made the call to dispatch. But I was convinced the man was dead. I shakily bent down to check for a pulse; there was none. I was going to try CPR, but I saw that his head was cocked at an unnatural angle to his body and his eyes were hooded and staring. Then there was an unholy shriek from behind me. I turned and saw the tiny woman, the one he had beaten nearly to a pulp, standing at the corner of the building, tearing at the stucco with her nails in a paroxysm of blind grief.

Glen, shaken by her display, moved toward her to try to comfort her. It was then that I realized we were not alone in the courtyard. Men and women, those who had merged with the shadows and watched us as we cruised by, were now moving toward us, encircling us, like zombies in some horror movie. The frigid wind tore at my hair and pricked my face, and it felt as if my blood had run cold. Then the small woman started screaming.

"They threw my baby out the window! They killed my baby boy!"

The impassive faces in the crowd became suffused with anger. My shock at what she was saying turned to fear, a pervasive fear that shot through my guts. I grabbed my radio as Glen instinctively moved closer to me, his drawn gun in one hand, his Mace in the other.

"Control, 1-Charlie-34. Officers need help, suspect down, crowd hostile. Officers need help."

Almost instantaneously I heard the wail of sirens rising over the screams of the woman inciting the crowd to "kill the police like they killed my baby boy!" The crowd surged forward. I raised my gun. Glen was next to me yelling, "Get back! Get back!" Then the whole courtyard erupted in blue and red flashing lights, which bounced off the buildings and illuminated the faces of the crowd. Cops were arriving from all over the city; I was never so glad to see uniforms in my life.

The crowd backed up as the patrol cars drove up onto the grass and walkways, disgorging cops with their batons and pistols drawn. Yellow crime scene tape was strung up around the entire courtyard, the thin fluttering plastic effectively separating them from us like a border between two hostile countries. The crowd remained, though, silent, watching as the paramedics pronounced the suspect dead and fled back to the safety of their rig. The crowd was still watching as the bosses arrived, having been yanked out of the warmth of their beds by urgent phone calls.

Glen and I retreated to the apartment, where a couple of detectives were talking to the small woman. Our sergeant, a veteran cop who had worked the streets for many years, met us and motioned us away. We followed him outside to where his patrol car was parked, its pulsing red and blue overheads reflecting off our faces.

"This could get ugly," he said without preamble. "Homicide and internal affairs are on the way. She's saying you threw him out the window."

Glen and I both began talking at once, defending ourselves, but he silenced us by raising his hand.

"I know it's bullshit," he assured us. "But both of you know the drill—I can't even ask you conversationally what happened, so just keep your heads and tough it out, okay?"

Glen couldn't keep his mouth shut, though; his frustration was boiling over. "Just look at her, Sarge! He was beating the shit out of her! He dove out the fucking window all by himself!"

The sergeant motioned for Glen to keep it down, but he kept it up. "Christ, Sarge, you know how these boyfriend/girlfriend things go. One minute he's kicking her ass and the next minute they're loving it up!"

The sergeant looked at the ground for a moment before his tired eyes met mine.

"You two read this one wrong. He was her son."

We both turned to look back at her as if that explained it all, but we were still dazed and bewildered by what had transpired. The next thirty minutes were a blur as the crime scene techs, more detectives, and the brass showed up. Glen and I stood off to one side; we'd been separated by the detectives and were not allowed to talk to each other. The silent crowd had not dispersed but stood staring at Glen and me with open hostility, and the curt glances we got from our coworkers were not reassuring. The wind whipped around me, stinging my face with missiles of sand and dirt, and I realized that my teeth were chattering as the detectives led me away to their unmarked car. Cop or suspect, I was no longer sure.

JUVENILE

BEING A COP MEANS BEING DEATH'S DANCE PARTNER. YOU
spend years getting to know its every move and countermove,
you learn to anticipate its every swing and dip and twirl, but just
when you think you've got it figured, it throws a new move at
you and you find yourself stumbling across some bloodstained
floor, an awkward neophyte in the brutal arms of a tango master.
Or that's what it seems like. When whirling out of control, some
of us pull our weapon and open fire; others just break from the
stiff embrace and walk away, leaving the dance hall days behind.
One thing is for certain: In every call in which Death lurks in
the background, the outcome will depend on which officers
respond.

That's not what any of us want to believe, is it? We all hope
that the end result of any given tragedy is as irrevocable as destiny and that the actors, criminals and police officers alike,
merely perform their role, their dance, according to some prede-
termined choreography—but that's just not the way it is.

"All units in the area of Alta and Decatur, report of an armed
robbery in progress at the clothing store. Suspect is armed with

what appears to be a machine gun and has a stocking mask over his head. Any unit that can respond, please advise."

That's how it began, my invitation to the dance with the juvenile. At the time, I'd been a cop for a good many years; if I hadn't, maybe somebody would be alive today who isn't. Or maybe someone else would be dead. Or maybe my rookie, sitting beside me with his eyes wide with alarm, would still be around. If, if, if . . . that's the purgatory of hindsight.

It was about 8:00 P.M. on a breezy autumn night. The glitz of the Las Vegas Strip wasn't visible from west of Industrial Road unless you were willing to drive a few miles. Our sector beat was mostly light industrial and commercial nestled within some low-income residential housing projects. My rookie was a second-career thirty-five-year-old fresh out of the academy, who kept looking with longing toward the neon-haloed horizon as if he could make the casino chorus-line dancers appear at will to add some glamour to these depressing backstreets. It was a look I'd seen before and one I must have had as a rookie cop seeking that glamour myself, but that was a long time ago. Right now I was hungry and starting to get cranky because we were too busy running call to call on this Friday night to get cleared for our dinner break. I don't work or play well with others when my stomach is growling, so I was just about to call the sergeant to pitch my complaint when the urgent tones of the emergency signal burst out of the radio.

I found myself smiling as I hit my bar lights. A call like that, as hot as any cop could ask for, provides an adrenaline rush that completely annihilates hunger, so my mood immediately improved.

"Did she say he's got a *machine gun?*" my rookie asked me. His pucker factor must have been off the chart, because his voice was tremulous, high-pitched.

"Any unit that can respond, please advise," repeated the dispatcher.

"Tell dispatch we've arrived," I said as I turned down the street bordering the shopping center where the robbery was going down. My rookie just stared at me as he watched me turn the lights off; I grabbed the mike myself.

"Control, 3-William-34 arrived," I radioed to dispatch before I turned to him. "Take a couple of deep breaths, okay? You take the shotgun and just follow my lead."

As I guided the dark patrol car across the parking lot toward the storefront, my rookie's shaking hand shot out for the button that would release the twelve-gauge pump shotgun from its perch on the console. And so the dance began.

I exited the vehicle and, with my .45 in my hand and extended downward, I moved quickly in soldier's jog toward the store, my rookie at my heels. The light from the plate glass window poured out onto the dark sidewalk: Every light was on inside the store. There was a lowrider car idling out in front, a chopped maroon Impala, with no one visible inside.

"Take up a position and cover the door," I whispered to my rookie, pointing to a cement column on one side of the store. "I'll check the car."

He peeled off, and I moved in a combat crouch toward the Impala, my .45 leading the dance. Nobody was ducked down inside the car; nobody was using it for cover. From my position next to this idling vehicle, in a miasma of exhaust fumes, I had a good view inside the clothing store.

It was like a framed theatrical scene: The shop was the stage, and I was an audience member in a darkened auditorium. The ongoing drama inside, on that supernatural stage, was brutal. A man wearing a stocking over his head was slamming a machine pistol into the face of a young Asian woman kneeling next to an open cash register. Before I could make a move, the woman slid to the floor and the gunman started running toward the front of the store. He had his machine pistol in one hand and a paper bag full of money in the other, and he was headed straight toward me. I could see him clearly; he had no idea that I was standing just outside the door in the dark.

I stepped away from the car and stood in a shooting stance. I lined up the groove of my .45 and started easing down on the trigger. *Shoot him,* the voice in my head was saying. *As soon as he pops his fucking head out of the door, shoot him. Don't give him the chance to open up with that machine gun.* I fully intended to do just that until I happened to glance over at my rookie, who was staring at me from behind the concrete pillar with an expression that looked a lot like fear. The gunman burst through the door. Before I could put the hammer down, I heard my own voice shouting.

"Police! Drop it now!"

And he did. The machine gun went flying down the sidewalk, and Stocking Head threw himself down on his knees while crying, "Don't shoot! Don't shoot!" The sonovabitch knew the drill and couldn't get rid of his gun fast enough.

"Face down on the ground! Hands away from your body! Now!" I was still shouting, and he was still screaming, "Don't shoot!" as he lay spread eagle on the sidewalk.

I kept him covered and tried to shake the feeling that I *had* opened fire when he came out of the door and that now he was lying dead on the ground, one less pistol-whipping punk alive on the planet. I glanced at my rookie, who was pie-eyed, sweat glistening on his face, the muzzle of the shotgun pointed down at the prostrate gunman.

"Cover me!" I shouted as I pulled out my cuffs. I moved over to

Stocking Head, straddled his prone figure, and jerked his hands behind his back, latching the cuffs as tight as they would go.

"Watch him while I check on the clerk!" I yelled to the rookie as I ran into the store. The Asian woman was huddled into a fetal position, moaning, blood pouring out of a gash on her cheek that extended up into her hairline. I yanked my radio off my belt and brought it up to my lips.

"Control, 3-William-34, roll medical for clerk. She's bleeding from a head wound." Before I could say more, I heard a moan from behind the counter. I leaned over to look and found another woman, an older, gray-haired version of the first clerk, lying in a pool of blood. She'd been pistol-whipped, too, and I could see where the blows had made craters in her skull.

"Control, 3-William-34, be advised we have two victims!" I shouted into my radio. Then I heard a tinkling as the door opened, and I whirled, raising my gun. It was just another cop, a guy I knew from roll call, carrying a first aid kit. I lowered my weapon, and we both looked down at the bloody woman convulsing on the floor in front of us.

"You've got this?" I asked as he knelt beside the woman. "I have to go check on the suspect." He nodded as he gently held the injured woman down by her shoulders to keep her thrashing head from cracking on the hard floor. I pushed out the door.

The light from the store still spilled out onto the sidewalk, and my rookie had crept into it. He was moving toward the gunman on the ground like a predator in a trance. The shotgun was extended like a divining rod, and in seconds he had the muzzle lodged against the back of the suspect's head and was whispering, "Don't make me do it . . . don't make me do it . . . don't make me do it . . ."

"Holy shit," I muttered. The rookie was going to blow the

gunman's brains all over the sidewalk. What had happened during the minute I was inside the store?

I made my expression blank and my voice reasonable and matter-of-fact. "Relax," I said. "He's not going anywhere."

The rookie looked up at me, sweat streaming down his face, the shotgun quivering in his grip.

"Give me the shotgun," I said gently, and reached out to pry it from his grasp.

"Don't shoot me!" wailed the gunman, his face on the pavement, his hands cuffed behind his back.

The rookie looked up at me blankly; it took a few seconds for him to register that I was there. He swallowed hard a few times, and as his grip loosened I took the weapon out of his hands.

"Go sit in the car," I told him. I must have sighed, because he looked at me closely, his eyes welling up with tears. "Go ahead," I offered. "I've got this."

The rookie turned away, stumbling off into the darkness toward the patrol car, leaving me alone with the suspect.

I squatted down on the dirty cement beside Stocking Head, my .45 just inches from the back of his head. I thought about the clerks inside the store. One or both probably suffered some brain damage. Maybe they wouldn't even live through this. "Don't make me do it," I whispered to the back of his head, wanting him to feel fear, as I checked him for additional weapons. Then I rolled him over on his back.

"Let's see the big man behind the mask," I said, my .45 trained on his stocking-obliterated features. With one fluid but not gentle motion I yanked the stocking off his head.

We stared into each other's eyes for what seemed like a long time. He was smiling. What I felt that moment was unlike anything that I've ever felt before or since. Regret, horrible regret. He was a stone killer, his eyes were completely devoid of any humanity, and I'd let him live.

His lips curled up into a mocking grin.

"I should have killed you when I had the chance, mother-fucker."

Those words I'll never forget, though I don't know which one of us actually said them aloud. I stood up and stared down at him, wondering if it was too late for me to get away with shooting him. But I'd missed my moment; such thoughts were nothing but a fantasy. As if to punctuate this, another patrol car came roaring up, and the sergeant jumped out and strode over. He looked at me, looked at my finger on the trigger on my .45, and then looked down at the suspect.

"Jesus Christ!" he said as he bent down. "How old are you?"

"Thirteen, motherfucker. How old are you?"

The sergeant gave me a questioning look before he headed into the store. "Jesus Christ!" was all he said.

Medical arrived and transported the critically injured women to the hospital. More cops showed up, as did the detectives and crime scene investigators. A pair of patrolmen took charge of the suspect. I holstered my weapon and carted the shotgun back to the patrol car, where I found the rookie sitting with the windows rolled up, staring straight ahead. I could see that he'd been crying. He didn't move when I opened the car door; he didn't flinch when I put my hand on his shoulder.

"Did you hear how old he was?" he asked me.

"Old enough to pull a trigger."

"He was thirteen."

"That's old enough to pull a trigger."

"The same age as my son," he said, and then looked at me. "My son is thirteen."

I looked back toward the store, remembering the malevolence in those eyes.

"He's nothing like your son."

"I'm done. All done."

I looked at him closely, trying to read the odd expression in his eyes.

"What do you mean?"

He unhooked his badge from his uniform shirt and, without looking at it, handed it to me.

"All done," he said again as he got out of the car. He un-snapped his gun belt, tossed it onto the seat, and walked away. I watched him go; he was headed in the direction of the police station a few blocks away. I wanted to run after him and lead him back to the handcuffed suspect and have him look into the void where the juvenile's eyes should have been.

"He's not like your son" was all I could say, but he was already out of sight.

EPILOGUE. The kid had lied about his age. He was really eleven. When I booked him into juvenile detention, I realized that just the year before I had arrested his father. For murder. Stocking Head Sr. was serving a life sentence, but he had already gotten his revenge on society. He had unleashed his perverted progeny, and it was coddled by the lenient laws for juvenile offenders. The juvenile had robbed and beaten two unarmed and unresisting salesclerks and had blinded one permanently. For this he was given eighteen months at youth camp.

I made it my business to keep track of the juvenile over the next couple of years, probably to confirm what I already knew. It was just three months after he was released from youth camp that he broke into an elderly neighbor's house. She was home at the time but posed no threat: She was confined to a wheelchair. That didn't give him pause, apparently, for he set upon her and stabbed her multiple times, leaving her bleeding on the floor. She lived for a couple of months before she died of complications from the stab wounds.

This time the juvenile was tried as an adult and sentenced to life in prison without the possibility of parole. I showed up for the sentencing hearing and noted that there was no one there except for the lawyers, a couple of court buffs, and a junior crime reporter. And my former partner, the rookie. I sat down beside him on the bench. I was in my uniform, he was in his civilian clothes, but when the juvenile turned around to be led out of the courtroom by the court officers, he recognized us—and laughed.

"Don't make me do it!" he hissed in falsetto as he passed us by. We both could hear him laughing all the way down the hallway.

The rookie looked older to me, as if he were carrying a burden that would not let him sleep.

"I almost . . ." He didn't finish.

"But you didn't," I insisted.

He nodded a couple of times, swallowed, and nodded again.

"I'm so glad I didn't," he said as he stood up and rested his hand on my shoulder briefly before he disappeared.

Not me, I thought. To this day I wish I had.

DEAD MAN TALKING

LAST NIGHT I TALKED TO A DEAD MAN. FORTUNATELY FOR HIM, he didn't know it. That he was dead, I mean. Of course, he wasn't dead yet, he was just in the process, or in transition, or in limbo, or whatever you'd call it.

I don't know how he would characterize our brief conversation, but for some reason I took special notice of the blood seeping through the knees of my uniform pants as I knelt beside him while trying to get him to tell me who had shot him in the back. In those suspended moments we were as intimate as lovers. My lips were close to his ear, whispering. I breathed in the scent of his cologne, tempered by the stench of death yet unfulfilled.

"Who did this to you?" I asked, almost whispering. "Who shot you?"

The white fishing cap was still on his head, pulled down low over his bushy eyebrows. One rheumy eye was half closed; the other seemed to crawl across my face. His black curly beard twitched and quivered as he answered in a throaty whisper.

"Ask my son."

I looked around, but there was nobody else. We were at the

end of his long cement driveway, halfway between his back door and his ramshackle garage, and just a few feet from his dented Chevy pickup truck. He must have been fishing that afternoon: Gear and tackle were propped up against an Igloo cooler and a couple of oversized buckets. The flashing red-and-blues of my cruiser hadn't attracted anybody's attention. We were all alone back there.

"Was your son here when you were shot?" I asked, hoping to be able to find a witness.

His white T-shirt was stained crimson and stuck to his back, the torn fabric creeping into the yawning entry wound. I didn't want to move him; the paramedics were on their way, but the spreading pool of blood, now looking like a small lake surrounding an inert and fleshy island, told me I didn't have much time to find out what had happened.

"Does your son know who shot you?"

The light in his one open eye began to fade, and I stepped up and away as a young paramedic materialized and slid an orange trauma board next to him. Two other rescue unit paramedics leaned down, their latex gloves making them look like dancers in a Berlin cabaret, and turned him over onto the board. The exit wound in the middle of his chest was the size of a man's fist, and I watched helplessly as great globs of lung tissue plopped onto the dirty cement. The dead man began gasping, his mouth moving, but no oxygen was able to find its way into his bloodstream; he looked like a fish that had been reeled in and dropped unceremoniously on the deck of a boat, its gills working feverishly in some futile effort to prolong its life a few moments more.

I watched the paramedics rush him to the waiting rig, feeling his blood cooling where it had soaked into my pants, when I heard the scrape of a match on the other side of the pickup truck. I had my gun leveled at his chest when my flashlight illu-minated and flattened his features. He had the same eyebrows as the dead man, the same reluctant chin. He'd been cleaning fish. Half a dozen undersized bass lay on the bloody cement at his feet amid their own scales and guts. The .45 was beside him on the folding deck chair, but he didn't reach for it; he didn't move. He just looked down at the cigarette in his hand and watched the smoke curl into the shadows. I didn't feel like asking him anything, so I just cuffed him and drove him in, thinking all the way about my conversation with the dead man, seized once again by a feeling of helplessness that seemed, appropriately, to hook itself into the soft flesh of my inner cheek and radiate out from there.

SHADOW OF THE EXECUTIONER

A CALM SPRING BREEZE WAFTED IN FROM THE PATROL CAR'S
window as I cruised through a neighborhood of comfortable
ranch-style houses. The sun that reflected off the hood of my
black-and-white was muted, nowhere near the fireball it would
become in a month or so, when the Las Vegas summer would
pounce with a vengeance. It was midafternoon, and I was doing a
solo beat on a lazy Sunday. The radio had been quiet all morning;
it was just too beautiful a day for trauma, but I'd been a street cop
for eighteen years and knew that misery could be just a radio
transmission away. Surrendering to the mood of the day, I made
the momentous decision of choosing Starbucks over 7-Eleven for
a cup of coffee. Maybe the last day of my workweek would, for
once, turn out to be uneventful. Then the dispatcher's dispas-
sionate voice pulled me out of my reverie.

"3-Baker-34, Control, copy a call MCT."

That wasn't a big deal; the code was for a nonpriority call, and
the details would be sent to my mobile computer terminal. If the
call had been "hot," an emergency or a crime in progress, the dispatcher would have given me some of the information over the

radio in order to shorten the response time, if only by seconds. The call flashed across my screen, giving me the address and details. I was to "check the welfare" of the caller's thirty-year-old son, Paul. The mother lived out of state and was concerned because he had been depressed and out of contact with her. He had not answered the phone for several days, and this was, according to her, very unusual. I acknowledged the call and pushed my en route button, which created a permanent record of the response time.

Whenever I heard the words "check the welfare," my senses came alive. Too many of these calls ended in the caller's worst nightmare: with a body in an empty house. Other times there was an irate relative who just wanted to be left alone. The fact is, when a cop walks up to any house to answer a "check the welfare" call, he has to be prepared for anything, especially the unexpected.

The address belonged to a small run-down house in the middle of a working-class neighborhood in a dusty cul-de-sac off Industrial Road. I parked a couple of doors down and watched the house for a few moments while finishing my coffee, scrutinizing my areas of cover and retreat should the worst happen. The front bay window was behind a recessed porch. A faded patchwork quilt had been tacked over the glass, and a dozen fliers for takeout restaurants lay fading on the porch. The house looked deserted, but for some reason I had a bad feeling about this one. I unsnapped the holster of my .45, my thumb having made that same trip a thousand times in the past. I breathed in the fresh springtime air and felt the gentle breeze blow against my face as I approached the front door and found that, behind the peeling wood-framed screen, it was wide open. Something wasn't right. It was too quiet. It was as if I could hear someone breathing along with the settling of the old house and smell someone lurking rank and watchful just beyond the shadows of the front door. I stepped to the side of the door and rapped hard on the wood frame. I waited; there was no response.

"Police officer. Paul, are you in there?"

Again I waited, but there was no sound from inside the house. I was about to go around to the back when I heard a man's disembodied voice. It seemed so close that I took a step backward.

"Come in, officer."

I froze. My threat antennae crackled, and I tried to isolate where the strange voice had come from. I could see a few feet into the darkened foyer, but there was no one there. He could only be standing deep in the shadows of the hallway to the back of the house. I couldn't see him, but I could feel him, and his voice riveted me. I heard something in it, something I had not heard as often as I had heard anger or fear or frustration; it was resignation. It was the voice of someone already dead.

"Is that you, Paul?" I asked, trying to get as much cover as I could at the side of the doorway.

"Yes . . . it's me," he replied quite softly, as if he weren't sure. Then his voice changed suddenly. Bitterness bubbled to the surface. "Come on in. What are you waiting for?"

"Paul, are you okay? You don't have any weapons, do you? No guns or bombs, right?" I asked as lightly as I could.

He didn't reply. I heard him cough spasmodically for several seconds and then moan softly.

"Are you okay, Paul?"

His voice grew shrill, plaintive. "Oh, for godsakes, come on in, I can't hurt you."

Did I believe him? Instinct drove me forward, and I took hold of the tarnished brass door handle and pulled it toward me while I kept my right hand on the butt of my .45. As the door swung open, I could see beyond the musty living room a kitchen with a scuffed and cracked green linoleum floor. I crossed the tattered carpet slowly and stood in the kitchen doorway. A faded white Formica dinette set with metal-framed chairs cushioned by broken plastic seat covers dominated the space. The cabinets were painted lime green, greasy with age. Unwashed pots and dishes, crusted and putrid with dried chili-from-a-can, were stacked on the counters. I took a few more steps and saw that the kitchen opened up to a small den where the dark fake-cherrywood paneling made the room seem even smaller than it was, humid, airless, and smelling of decay. Paul was sitting, slumped to one side, on a worn camel-colored couch in front of an old coffee table camouflaged by countless prescription pill bottles.

I stepped to the side of the door so that I could see him better and to reduce my silhouette against the background of that suffocating place. He blinked, trying to see me in the shadows. He was clad in a soiled white sleeveless T-shirt and wrinkled hospital scrubs. His longish brown hair was lank and unwashed, and his skinny arms and face were punctuated by ulcerated sores. His complexion was sallow; his bruised brown eyes spoke of unrelenting pain.

He smiled, head cocking slightly to one side, yellowed teeth visible through several days' growth of sparse beard. "Quite a sight, huh, officer?"

I made no comment.

"Did my mother send you?" he asked.

"Yes, she did, Paul. She's concerned about you and wanted us to make sure you're all right."

He didn't say anything at first; he just leaned forward again, looking at me, looking almost through me, his eyes so full of pain that it was almost palpable. He locked his gaze onto mine and asked softly, "Do you know what it's like to die?"

For a moment, I felt as if we were far away from that slovenly hovel, as if I were a lone soldier coming across a dying man on a muddy battlefield. He really wanted to know the answer; his question wasn't rhetorical.

"No, Paul, I don't," I answered him honestly. "I've seen death many times, but I don't really know it at all."

His eyes would not leave mine, and I couldn't tear mine away from his. Then tears spilled over and ran down his jaundiced cheeks. A strange smile flirted with the corners of his cracked lips.

"You will help me, won't you?"

His question fractured my reverie, and I stepped back. I watched in fascination as the tears seemed to leave welts from his eyes to his chin.

"Do it," he whispered. "Please do it."

His plea cut through me, chilling me, and suddenly I felt a disorienting, almost dizzying sensation, because I realized he had read my mind. I forced my hand away from my gun as if by removing its proximity I could remove even the remnants of that horrible fleeting thought from my consciousness. His haunted eyes bore into me, focusing on me as his liberation.

"I can't," I heard myself say. I almost didn't recognize my own voice. "I can't," I repeated, trying to convince myself more than him.

"Please, please . . . I'm begging you."

He actually slid off the couch and onto his bony knees in a gesture of supplication. I recoiled and yet at the same moment visualized my pistol jumping in my hand, the muzzle flash, the smoke. The slow-motion explosion of blood and flesh, his tormented body limp, his tortured essence liberated at last, taking flight toward whatever spiritual plane awaited him. I was no stranger to taking a human life, but this would be something far different. This would be murder . . . or would it? I realized he was smiling at me. I also realized that my hand was once again on the butt of my gun. My face felt aflame, and I tore my hand away; I stepped backward into the fetid kitchen. My left hand sought out my portable radio.

"Control, 3-Baker-34, roll medical."

Paul sank back onto the couch, his face expressionless, waxen. He didn't look at me again. When the paramedics arrived, I left immediately, fleeing not only the dying man but also my own lingering shadow, the shadow of the executioner.

THE JOURNEY

THE STEEL BARS OF THE COUNTY JAIL SLAMMED SHUT BEHIND
me with their customary cheerless finality as I trudged back to
my patrol car. The twenty-three-year-old tweaked-out stripper I
had just booked on a narcotics charge was my third arrest of the
shift. When she had learned that her impressive display of sili-
cone accoutrements was not going to keep her from a felony
dope rap, she had let loose with a well-aimed phlegm missile, and
now I felt like steam-cleaning my face. All I wanted to do was
grab a cup of hot coffee, head back to the station, park myself in
an office, finish my paperwork, and stop for a couple of beers on
the way home.

The blazing afternoon sun stabbed into my eyes as I crawled
along with traffic, impatiently drumming my fingers against the
steering wheel. I looked at my face in the rearview mirror. My
cheek was abraded where I had wiped off the wad of spittle. Getting spat on was my least favorite form of nonverbal communica-
tion, and I had reined myself in from bitch-slapping her; it was a
fitting end to another lousy day. I had every intention of putting
on the blinders that every cop keeps handy when he doesn't want

to get involved with people. I felt the cumulative effect of twenty years of pushing a black-and-white around the sweltering city while being a frontline witness to the carnage, greed, and general nastiness that the people we try our damnedest to serve and protect engage in on a daily basis. I was counting down the days until my pension liberated me from the job I had once been so proud of. Now I was just like the inmates in the county jail, counting down the days to my release.

Sitting there in traffic, I wondered what had happened to me. The things that had once given me simple joy and pleasure now failed to even pique my interest. The words of my last longtime girlfriend echoed in my head. She had packed up and moved out while I was working, leaving a note Scotch-taped to the bathroom mirror. It presented a detailed list of all my failings and ended by saying that I was "untouchable." Maybe she was right; I didn't care enough about her note to rip it off the mirror and ball it up or burn it or even preserve it as some poignant memento of lost love. I just pulled it off the glass so that I could see my face in the mirror and dropped it idly in the trash. That was nearly a year ago, and I hardly thought about her at all.

There was a coffee shop just up the road in the blue-collar neighborhood that I was driving through. I'd get a cup of coffee and use their bathroom to scrub my face one more time. I was about to turn down a side street when I saw her, a little girl of about eight walking alone. It triggered a memory: a little girl's broken body in a Dumpster, small rigid fingers clutching a stuffed teddy bear. Her hooded eyes were wide open, lifeless and dull, but staring straight through the young police officer I once was. I have long forgotten the details of the crime, but the murdered little girl's image has made guest appearances in my dreams for many years.

This little girl, the living one, was standing patiently on the corner just up ahead, waiting to cross the street while the never-ending river of cars flowed by. As I drove closer, I could see her more clearly. She didn't resemble the girl in the Dumpster at all except that she, too, was young and black. She had a milk chocolate complexion, and her long, dark hair had been pulled tightly into a ponytail cascading down her thin back. She was wearing what looked like the white blouse and plaid skirt of a school uniform; despite the chill in the October air, she wasn't wearing a jacket. She carried nothing with her but an air of perfect innocence. She looked up and down the street as she patiently waited for her chance to cross.

Without even thinking about what I was doing, I drove close to the corner and slowed to a stop, flicking on the overhead light bar of my unit to stop the traffic behind me. I wanted to give her the chance to cross, but she didn't step off the curb; for a moment she looked pensively across the wide intersection, and then her big eyes met mine. I got out of the patrol car and walked over to her, aware of the stares of the rush-hour commuters stopped behind me and of those passing from the opposite direction.

"May I walk with you across the street?" I asked, taking off my sunglasses and leaning down so that she could look me directly in the eyes.

She nodded shyly and reached out her hand as if we had crossed a hundred streets together. I took her small hand in mine and felt its warmth.

"My mommy always said that a policeman would help me," she whispered in a soft voice with a southern lilt, and her face lit up with a smile so pure and genuine that I felt something stir within me. She looked up at me, and we swung our arms slightly as we began our journey.

It was a magic moment: All the cars on the street, in all four corners of the intersection, slowed and stopped to watch our progress. Drivers, instead of being angry at the delay, were mesmerized by the sight of the uniformed cop walking hand in hand across the street with a little girl. I saw smiles on the faces of some that earlier I would have cynically pegged as suspects or parole violators. I felt something that I hadn't felt in a long time; I felt good inside.

Our journey ended much too quickly. As we stepped up onto the far curb, I released her little hand.

"Thank you, officer," she said, and gave me another incredible smile. Then she did something that so surprised me that I couldn't even react for a moment. She stood up on her tiptoes and threw her thin arms around my neck and hugged me.

"I love you, officer," she whispered with her soft cheek next to mine. There was no trace of anything in her tone but a little girl's truth. I hugged her back hesitantly and quickly let her go. I watched her for a moment as she walked away, then turned back toward my patrol car. I noticed that the traffic still wasn't moving, that the occupants of the stopped cars were all smiling, as if the image of the cop and the little girl had touched them in some way.

In that moment, as I stepped off the curb, I remembered why I had become a cop.

HER NAME WAS JACKIE

THE FOUR-YEAR-OLD COMPACT CAR WAS STOPPED AT THE traffic light. The neon lights from the casinos flashed their staccato rhythm and reflected on the faces of the family in the cool Las Vegas night. Times were getting better for the young couple. Steady work, a small home, and the addition of the little one-month-old baby girl now happily burbling in the infant seat gave the young family hope that the American Dream might just become a reality. They were on their way to the store to pick up some formula and diapers. The new father glanced over to watch as his young wife turned around in her seat to stroke the baby's face with the back of her hand. He smiled as he returned his concentration to driving and was just about to ease down on the accelerator in anticipation of the light turning green. He had no reason to pay any attention to the lowered primer-gray Buick idling next to them.

The shaved heads of the two men inside the Buick glistened with sweat even though the brisk winter nights in Las Vegas had people donning their coats. The cocaine surging through their systems had raised their body temperature and reduced their ability to think or feel. There was no reason to do what they did next. They shared the ethnic heritage of the young couple, but certainly not their values, not their hopes. Maybe that void was why they chose that moment to raise their 9 mm semiautomatics and empty them into the car beside them. The bullets tore into the glass and metal, devastating everything in their path.

In the four-year-old compact, the baby, who moments before had been innocently waving her little arms in the air, enveloped in the warmth and love of parents who adored her, now lay motionless. She was still strapped into her car seat, but now blood was pouring from the horrible gash where the bullet had ripped into her face. The mother screamed as shards of glass imploded into the car while the father punched the gas pedal in a frantic attempt to escape the fusillade. Without a backward glance the two gang punks sped off, laughing, proud of the "courage" it took to indiscriminately open fire on the innocent, not giving a damn.

My patrol car glided through the night on a collision course with this family's destiny. I had more than twenty years of experience behind the badge, but this night I would always remember. I was first alerted that something was wrong when I approached the intersection and saw the compact car parked at a weird angle. I noticed the panicked, jerky movements of the people surrounding it before I heard a woman screaming. As I climbed out of my unit, I heard someone yell, "My God, my God, the baby's been shot!" It was then that I saw the infant car seat on the sidewalk next to the car. My flashlight illuminated the tiny face awash with blood, and my heart fell as I saw the little body jerking spasmodically.

I was alone on this call. I needed three heads and ten hands. Who shot her? Were they still nearby? I needed to get medical attention for the baby. Procedure is clear: Summon the paramedics and begin the investigation. But people were shouting, crying, and all I could think of was that I must help the baby. I radioed for assistance, but as I knelt beside her, I found she wasn't breathing. Then, as if in answer to a prayer, another patrol car pulled up. It was all instinct after that—I didn't give another thought to procedure. I snatched up the limp and bloody bundle, jumped into the front seat, and shouted to the young cop to get to the hospital. As I cradled the infant in my arms I saw that the bullet had inflicted so much damage on her tiny face that she was choking on her own blood and tissue. I scooped out the gory pulp with my fingers and then, knowing that the baby had no chance of surviving otherwise, I began mouth-to-wound resuscitation. I sealed my mouth over her devastated mouth and nose and began to breathe my life into her little lungs. I prayed between breaths, "Please, little one, please live." The young cop next to me drove like Mario Andretti; without a moment's hesitation, my mission to save this tiny child had become his.

We hurtled through dark alleys, down neon-lit boulevards, as the siren pulsed and the flashing reds and blues reflected off the buildings. I continued to breathe life into the baby's lungs, and in a few moments—or was it a lifetime?—I heard the most beautiful sound in the world . . . a baby crying. I had tempted her back from whatever dark place she had traveled to. I tasted her blood on my lips. In any other circumstances I would have been repelled by this gory intimacy, but at this moment I only felt an incredible surge of blessed joy. I believed she had come back for me. As I held that child and urged her to stay with me through my whispered entreaties, my silent pleas to God, I felt the pull of a bond that would never be torn asunder. My life and that of this tiny girl had collided and meshed in some prophetic way.

The trauma team was waiting at the hospital, and I handed off my precious charge to those who would now shoulder the responsibility for her life. They hustled her away. I felt my heart pounding beneath my Kevlar vest. I tasted my tears before I even knew I was crying. I prayed as I silently watched the trauma team work their magic.

Maybe those prayers were heard and answered: I looked up and saw the trauma team nurse approaching me . . . smiling. She said that the little girl was going to make it. She would need extensive cosmetic surgery in the future to hide the terrible scars that would be a constant reminder of this nightmare come true. I had a last glimpse of the tiny, fragile girl as the masked and scrubs-clad figures huddled over her in the stark light. That image has stayed in my mind: The tragic reality of what had happened would never be clearer than at that moment.

As I walked out of the treatment area I heard an accented voice say, "That's him! That's the one!" I turned and saw the young couple whose nightmare I had shared. They ran toward me and thanked me in two different languages for saving their baby. It was only then that I learned that her name was Jackie. I had no words; I could only silently wrap my arms around the both of them. The mother looked up at me and, seeing her daughter's blood on my face, reached up and touched it wonderingly with the tips of her fingers. I will never know what thoughts ran through her mind at that moment. I only know that as her fingers drifted away, her tears ran silently down her cheeks even as she tried to show her gratitude with a shaky smile. I could feel my own eyes start to burn, so I walked away and walked out of the hospital, back into the cool Las Vegas night, back to work.

EPILOGUE. Little Jackie was shot in February 1998. Shortly after the incident, I opened a bank account for the injured infant, and the Las Vegas community rallied behind her recovery. A local radio station raised $4,000 in just one day for Jackie's medical expenses. Entertainers contributed generously. The Hilton Hotel donated two nights of nightclub receipts totaling near $20,000, and the medical community donated much of the surgical costs. Jackie was to endure multiple reconstructive surgeries, but the happy little girl now bears only a tiny scar as a memento of that horrible night—a night that brought the lives of an infant, a family, a veteran cop, and, ultimately, a city together.

THE ULTIMATE
NINJA WARRIOR

MANY YEARS HAVE PASSED SINCE THE NIGHT I KILLED SOMEONE.
I have spent those years as any man might, seducing life with wild
abandon while my companions cheered me on. I seized each moment for what it was—an unrepeatable experience, whether it be
physical or sensual or, to a lesser extent as time went by, emotional. I always thought that I was propelled into living intensely
by my pleasure-seeking nature, but now, as I more and more
shun the company of others and live as a recluse, as loneliness
has taken the place of my companions, as I undertake a seden-
tary life that I don't recall having volunteered for and which I still
don't accept as belonging to me, I have begun to reflect, and to
reflect with brutal honesty. All the roads in my long life seem to
lead back to that one night when I took a human life.

Perhaps I have gotten ahead of myself, for in describing the results of an act I have omitted the event itself. If my plea for empathy is to have any merit at all, then the facts must be included
for you to draw your own conclusions. Facts, unadulterated,
speak insistently for themselves, and as a veteran cop I have
spent a lifetime working with nothing but facts. How you will

regard these facts is up to you; I can only describe that night as I remember it.

Las Vegas is known to the world as the mecca of hedonism. It is "Sin City," the capital of abandoned inhibitions, the neon bacchanalia where appetite dominates reason. For nearly half a century her pulsating lights have hypnotized her acolytes, luring them into her world of gambling, gluttony, and sexual pleasures. It is a world that most have only fantasized about. She is all she promises to be; what is rumored to be not only exists but flourishes beyond the wildest imagination. What isn't known, what isn't celebrated, is the parallel universe that exists beyond those neon sentinels, the same world of placid neighborhoods and shopping centers that dominates our nation's suburban sprawl. The same domestic melodramas erupting on a Saturday night after too many beers, the same youthful exuberance gone awry by way of a speeding minivan full of teenagers—these exist in the figurative back lot of Las Vegas just as they do in all our major towns and cities. It was within this unassuming reality, contained within a larger-than-life reality, that one man sought me out to end his life.

He was delusional. He heard voices. He believed that he had been appointed as an avenger, a liberator through death. He had lived with demons for a long time and had given up trying to keep them at bay with medication and moderation. No matter how tightly he closed the shades in his mind, they kept slipping through, howling and keening, to prey like demonic leopards upon what was left of his reason. Finally he embraced his calling, and they, the ubiquitous carnivorous "they," christened him "the Ultimate Ninja Warrior." He prepared himself to accept his appointed role. He donned black karate gear, strapped a shoulder holster holding a stolen semiautomatic pistol to his body, draped himself with ammunition belts and a samurai sword, and headed to the high school dance.

The Ultimate Ninja Warrior was a young man, not much older than the teenagers attending the event. When he appeared like a specter out of the trees lining the athletic field that cool autumn night, most of the boys and girls laughed, thinking it was one of their classmates pulling a prank. As the black-clad figure approached the gymnasium, he opened fire. For a moment the young people stood frozen in disbelief, but as the windows began exploding all around them, they panicked, and terror fueled their chaotic rush to escape. The Ninja embraced this confusion and charged into the building, his semiautomatic pistol held like a triumphant banner in his hand. He kept firing.

The teenagers scattered in every direction, some falling and others, propelled by primal fear and survival instinct, clambering over them without trying to help. Overwhelmed and terrified, each lost a part of himself or herself as the hail of bullets blasted the brick walls and shattered the windows, leaving fragments of glass and brick to rain down upon them like wrath on Judgment Day.

Within moments of the first shots, a 911 operator received the first phone call. At first she thought that the breathless young woman on the other end of the line was making a prank call, but then she, too, heard the *pfffttt* sound of bullets exploding in the background. The other operators began receiving similar calls. Soon the urgent tone of an emergency broadcast was flying out over the radios of patrol cars across the city.

"All units in sector Union 3, a report of a shooting in progress at Torrey Pines High School. Caller reports that a male dressed in all black is armed with a pistol and is walking eastbound on Thrush Street shooting at students."

The dispatcher's voice was calm, but there was an edge to it that I could detect even before I turned up the volume on my portable radio. I had just left the diner and was walking with my former partner Dave and his young rookie. The three of us had eaten an enjoyable dinner, and we'd joked about what a quiet night it had been so far. We stood in the parking lot, listening to the dispatcher's summary of something that seemed more like the basis of a national news broadcast than an event transpiring in this quiet corner of the city.

"That's three blocks from here," I said, listening for the sound of gunfire.

"Sounds like bullshit to me," Dave said calmly, unwrapping a toothpick. "Some kind of prank call."

The rookie laughed nervously, nodding in hopeful agreement.

I laughed, too, but it was my sector, so I yanked the portable radio from the holster on my belt and told the dispatcher I was on my way. As I started to climb into my patrol car, Dave looked at me across the roof of his unit and said, "What the hell, we'll back you."

Since I was only about a minute away I didn't throw on my overheads, so I was flying dark as I punched the accelerator and screeched around the corner to where the shooter had last been seen. I could make out the lighted windows of the high school gymnasium up ahead, but so far nothing seemed out of the ordinary. Then I caught sight of another patrol car up ahead. Its brake lights came on as the dispatcher radioed that a man with a cellular phone who had been following the suspect had just been shot.

I pulled to a stop behind the patrol car as the two cops jumped out and used their open doors for cover. They both were pointing their pistols into the darkness, the tension evident in the arch of their backs. Then my headlights caught what they were aiming at: a figure striding toward them down the middle of the street. He was like a creature out of a low-budget horror movie— dressed from head to toe in a black ninja outfit, bandoliers of ammunition strapped across his chest and a pistol in his hand.

Shoot him! I thought, *shoot him before he gets too close to you— shoot him!* But the ninja didn't cross that invisible line that divides close from too close, and I watched him put his pistol back in his shoulder holster. Suddenly he turned and walked into the driveway of an apartment complex. The two cops stayed in position behind their patrol car doors, frozen, it seemed, with indecision. I didn't blame them; for a moment I wondered if I had seen what I thought I had. Then the police helicopter appeared overhead; my rocketing adrenaline made the blood pound so loudly in my ears that I didn't even hear it coming. Now there it was, so close that it was battering the palm trees all around us with its prop wash. It lit up the ninja with its powerful searchlight, and I made a dash for the trees lining the driveway of the apartment building, my 9 mm extended in my hand. As I ran, the staccato rhythm of the chopper blades in concert with the pulsing beam of the searchlight and the red and blue of the overhead lights of the first patrol car gave the confidently striding black-clad figure a demonic look.

I ran along the tree-lined path parallel with the driveway, almost alongside the ninja, shouting, "Police! Stop! Police!" I might as well have been talking to myself. He didn't look over at me; he didn't break his stride. I was starting to feel a sense of desperation. Since his gun was holstered, I didn't want to shoot him in the back, but people were beginning to emerge from their apartments, curious about the noise and lights from the helicopter overhead, and they were right in the path of the oncoming ninja.

I didn't have any choice, so I made the decision that will haunt me forever. I broke out of the bushes and ran up behind him, screaming at the top of my lungs to divert his attention from the people filling the apartment courtyard up ahead. He turned to look at me. In that same instant he drew his semiautomatic pistol from his shoulder holster and pointed it at my chest. My forward momentum wouldn't let me stop, and I plowed toward him while raising my own pistol and bringing my knee up to connect solidly with his torso. We both fired simultaneously, and as I was just three feet from him, I expected to feel his bullet searing through my body. But before anything could register, pain or fear, we both fired again.

Time stopped. The helicopter's searchlight was pulsing over us, the wind tore at my uniform, and the muzzle flashes looked like distant fireworks on the Fourth of July. Then my gun jammed—my worst nightmare; it had plagued my dreams for years. This madman, this ninja warrior, was standing only a yard away from me, still firing, and my gun wouldn't work. I had no cover, so I dropped to the ground and rolled, wondering if I was dead and just hadn't realized it. As I worked the slide of my gun, clearing the mechanism, he continued to fire. I rolled from side to side trying to avoid his aim. I fired again, but there was no reaction to my shots. I wasn't wearing any body armor; I wondered if he was.

Overhead the helicopter cops had seen the muzzle flashes and watched me fall to the ground. They thought I'd been shot. "Shots fired! Officer down!" a tinny voice screamed over the portable radio. The cops at the entrance to the apartment complex opened fire, thinking I'd been hit. I heard the bullets whizzing overhead as I struggled to my feet, trying to show the others I was all right.

I heard the roar of a powerful car engine, and out of the corner of my eye I saw a patrol car hurtling toward us, my old partner

Dave at the wheel, his face grim and determined. *He's going to run the sonovabitch over!* I thought, both amazed and absurdly grateful. The patrol car slammed into the cement divider that kept cars from driving into the apartment courtyard, the engine revving, the tires burning rubber, but he couldn't get through those impervious concrete blocks even by ramming them while accelerating. My dismay turned to fury when I saw that the Ninja was distracted. As he looked over at Dave behind the wheel of the smoking patrol car, I emptied my magazine into him.

It was insane: My hollowpoint rounds had no effect on him whatsoever. As I reloaded, his attention once again turned to me, and he fired, missing me thanks to what seemed like supernatural intervention. Then I heard Dave's boots pounding on the pavement as he ran toward us. Inexplicably, the Ultimate Ninja Warrior turned and ran.

I slammed another magazine into my gun, and Dave and I ran after him around the corner of the building while exchanging shots. "Die, motherfucker, die!" I heard a shrill voice from behind a bush screaming as we turned the corner, one peeling left, one right. "Die, motherfucker, die!" Then I saw the muzzle flash from behind the bush, and we both fired into it until a black-clad body rolled out. As Dave ran up to handcuff the figure, I covered him, ready at the slightest provocation to fire again. Dave turned him over.

The searchlight of the air unit illuminated the scene just as the disco ball had illuminated the high school dance floor before this black-clad assassin had destroyed what had been innocent and pristine. I bent down to look at him. His face mask had fallen to one side, and I saw to my surprise that he wasn't much older than those whose lives he sought to end. He was hardly more than a boy. His brown eyes were sightless, bulging, staring into mine. Half of his face had been shot away, and what was left was mocking and macabre. He seemed to be grinning, his face shining wetly with bloody froth.

I don't know how long I bent over him trying to reconcile what I saw on the ground with what had stood before me in a hail of muzzle flash, seemingly immortal. Finally I stood up and met Dave's eyes. He was staring at me with the strangest look on his face. Before I could say a word, the brass, internal affairs, crime lab techs, and dozens of curious cops surrounded us. As is required, they separated us—the two cops involved in the shooting—and a grizzled homicide detective led me to an unmarked car.

"You did good, son," he said. "You survived."

I did, didn't I? I thought. For the life of me, I didn't know how.

The next few hours were a blur. I gave a taped statement about the shooting to homicide, and I was relieved of my gun so that it could be checked by ballistics for malfunctions. When my inquisition was all over, I changed out of my uniform and went to a bar where I knew I'd find other cops. I didn't want to be alone, but when I found myself the center of attention, answering questions about the shooting from all the curious cops I worked with, I realized I didn't want to be there, either. I suddenly didn't feel like I belonged. Anywhere.

This officer-involved shooting happened a long time ago, but in many ways it seems as if it happened only yesterday. While the intervening years have brought me close to death on many subsequent occasions, that particular night left me with far more questions than answers. Most of my questions begin with "why." Why was I spared that night when by all rights I shouldn't have survived? Why was I the one chosen to end that disturbed boy's life? Why did our paths cross that night? Why do I have to bear this for the rest of my life?

A couple of months ago, I met my old partner Dave for drinks. Both of us are nearing retirement age and have seen our share of combat. We seldom talk about our encounter with the Ultimate Ninja Warrior, but for some reason our conversation turned back to that surreal autumn night. We relived it, play by play, consuming more alcohol than we should have. We started our path of remembrance from our dinner break with his young rookie in tow and ended with our turning the ninja's body over and regarding his devastated face. Then I caught that look again—the same one he had given me when I leaned down to get a good look at the dead man.

"What? Why are you looking at me like that?" I asked.

"It's nothing," he said, letting his eyes return to contemplating the reflective light on his glass of scotch.

"Bullshit, Dave."

He ran his fingers down the side of the glass, gathering moisture on his fingertips, then he looked over at me.

"When we chased Ninja-man around the corner of that building and found him hiding behind that bush . . ."

"Yeah?" I prompted.

"What do you remember?"

I felt the alcohol driving through me as the memory vividly played out in my mind. I could see it as if it had happened yesterday, every damn detail. I looked over at Dave.

"We came running around the corner, and as he screamed, 'Die, motherfucker, die!' we opened up on him." I shrugged. "Ninja-man was fucking crazy. End of story."

I took another swig of my scotch and emptied the glass. Dave was staring straight ahead, and I could see that he was looking at my reflection in the mirror above the bar.

"Will you fucking tell me what's on your mind, Dave?"

He turned toward me, swiveling on his stool.

"It was you."

I didn't get it. "What do you mean it was me?"

"You really don't know, do you?"

"Dave, will you please—"

"It was you. Ninja-man never said a word. It was you who yelled 'Die, motherfucker, die!' "

THE MAN OF THE HOUSE

I MET MARIA RODRIGUES ON THE NIGHT OF HER FIFTY-NINTH birthday, three hours before she was beaten to death with an empty "40-ouncer." It was 9:30 P.M. on a Friday, and patrol cars in every major city were jumping from call to call. It was no different in Las Vegas on the last night of Maria's life.

The apartment where she paid the rent was in the shadows of the Las Vegas Strip and pulsated with neon from dusk to dawn, but it was home to Maria, her thirty-year-old daughter, and her two grandchildren, José, nine, and Carmelita, six. It was also within my patrol beat, so when a disturbance was reported at Maria's apartment, I heard about it over the radio traffic.

Then I heard, "614, Control, can you copy a call? I'll get you backup as soon as a unit clears."

As a supervising sergeant I didn't normally handle routine calls, but everyone else in the sector was tied up, so I took a look at the details on my mobile computer: Some young men were causing a disturbance in an apartment complex. Apparently they were sitting on a utility box and were making noise and yelling and refusing to leave. This was according to the caller in apartment 101,

Maria Rodrigues. It sounded like a typical Friday night too-raucous "curb party." Nothing out of the ordinary.

"Control, 614, copy and en route to handle."

I pulled my black-and-white into the cul-de-sac where the apartment complex was located. I'd been out there on more than one occasion. These apartments catered to the government-subsidized Section 8 and welfare-recipient crowd but, surprisingly, were not a high crime area. Aside from some old cars perched on cinder blocks, empty Budweiser cans, and fast food wrappers rolling around like miniature paper tumbleweeds, the street was clean and relatively quiet.

The Hispanic woman who answered my knock at apartment 101 was plump, with a weathered face and long graying hair pulled back into a severe bun, but her smile was warm, even apologetic.

"Mrs. Rodrigues?"

She nodded. "Please, just Maria is fine. Officer, I'm sorry to have bothered you," she told me in heavily accented English before I could even ask a question. "The boys left about fifteen minutes ago."

Behind her I could see a little girl clinging tightly to her long black skirt, peeking around at me, her eyes wide with curiosity. A few feet behind her a young boy, just a few years older than his sister, stood very still and stared at me with a solemn expression. Maria started to close the door, but I stopped her and returned her smile.

"Why don't you tell me what happened," I said, and she opened the door wide and gestured for me to follow her into the living room. The room was tidy, and the aged but well-kept furniture seemed to belong in a formal parlor in another time and place, maybe Spain in the nineteenth century. It was all dark mahogany wood and rich plum brocade. What struck me was that there was no television set, only a worn leather-bound Bible in Spanish and a small shrine to the Virgin Mary complete with flickering votive candles. Despite its formality, the room was comfortable and welcoming. I sat on the couch; she sat across from me in a straight-backed chair.

"I was putting the children to bed."

"They're your children?"

"My grandchildren, yes."

"You take care of them?"

"They live with me. My daughter lives here, too, but tonight she is . . . out." She held my eyes with hers, deep obsidian eyes that filled suddenly with great sadness. "She goes to the bars . . . sometimes she doesn't come home."

"Ah . . . Okay. What happened tonight?"

"I was putting the children to bed, and these three boys were sitting outside on the electric box drinking beer." She gestured outside; I knew the utility box was just half a dozen feet from the open window. "They were talking so loud that the children could not sleep. So I asked them to speak softer." She hesitated for a moment and looked down at the floor.

"What did they do?"

"They cursed me. All I did was ask them to speak a little softer so that the children could sleep." She sat even straighter, defiance in her eyes. "I told them I would call the police . . . and I did."

I knew that for her to threaten to call the police wouldn't make her very popular with the Li'l Locos, the local gang that claimed this area as their own. I admired her courage.

Then she began to talk, telling me proudly about her two grandchildren: They were both bilingual, they both loved to read, and they both dutifully accompanied her to the Catholic church just across Paradise Road every Sunday. She called them over to introduce them. The little girl hid behind her grandmother's chair, not sure what to make of this strange man in uniform, while her brother walked closer, staring at the gun in my holster. I stood up and then squatted down so that I would be at eye level with the children.

"Hi, how are you guys doing?" The little girl, Carmelita, smiled before she ducked down behind her grandmother, but the little boy was braver. He stepped forward and stuck out his small hand. I shook it.

"My name is Randy. What's your name?"

"José."

"Are you taking good care of your grandmother, José?"

He glanced up at his grandmother, who was beaming proudly, and then back at me. His face erupted in the most beatific smile I had ever seen, and he nodded his head with great enthusiasm. I couldn't help but return the smile.

"Well, I can see that you're the man of the house."

As I headed back toward the front door, I caught sight of a birthday cake sitting at the center of a scarred wooden kitchen table. It looked like a confectionery pincushion with all the half-burned candles. Several slices were missing, and I noticed a large carving knife with a red handle on a nearby plate, its blade smeared with vanilla frosting. Maria touched my arm, stopping me before I crossed to the front door.

"It was my fifty-ninth birthday today," she told me proudly. "Would you like some cake?"

My portable radio was spitting out calls one after the other, but there was something about this little family that made me want to linger for just a few minutes longer. I wasn't hungry; I certainly wasn't interested in dessert, but I said, "Sure, I'd love a piece of cake."

The children followed me over to the table, their eyes never leaving me as I took a seat: As Maria cut me a slice of cake, I winked at Carmelita, and she fled down the hallway with a huge smile on her face, back to where I figured the bedrooms must be. José stood beside me, his eyes locked on the .45 at my hip. He pointed at the gun.

"Have you ever shot anybody?"

That's something that almost everybody wants to know but that only children are bold enough to ask.

"Only bad people," I answered honestly.

Then, just as Maria placed the plate in front of me, I heard my call sign over the radio advising me of a fatal traffic accident requiring a supervisor. I stood up and rogered the call.

"I've got to go," I told Maria, and then, as if I had to offer some sort of explanation, I said, "There's been a bad accident and they need me." I reached into my shirt pocket and retrieved a business card with my name and the police department phone number on it and placed it on the table next to the cake. "If you have any more trouble with those guys, just call and ask for me."

She glanced at the card and then looked up at me.

"Thank you for caring," she said in a soft voice.

José snatched the card off the table and stared at it, running his fingers over the prominent embossed gold badge. I ruffled his hair, and as he turned his eyes toward me I said, "You take care of your grandmother, okay? You're the man of the house." He was nodding solemnly as I walked out into the heat of the desert night.

My thoughts were occupied over the next few hours with the

carnage of the double fatal traffic accident out on Industrial Road and the constant calls for service. Finally, at around midnight, I was about to head in to take care of my paperwork when the radio tone alert signifying a high priority call caught my attention.

"All units, all units. Report of a possible stabbing at 2833 Hayes Street, apartment 101. Caller is a young Hispanic male who is saying that his grandmother is bleeding."

I was numb when I recognized Maria's address. I grabbed the radio mike and told dispatch as well as the other units that I would be riding on the call.

"Control, 614. Be advised that I was on a call earlier at that apartment. Three Latin males had threatened the caller but were gone on my arrival."

Seconds later dispatch announced, "614 and all units responding to the possible stabbing, be advised that medical is en route for the victim."

I felt the blood pounding in my ears as adrenaline pumped through me. My siren wailed urgently as the staccato rhythm of my red and blue lights reflected off the apprehensive faces of the motorists that I was flying past. As I used my radio to direct the arriving units to take up positions around the neighborhood in an effort to contain the suspects, I silently pleaded, *Please . . . please let them be okay.* I was just a few seconds away when I heard the words that I was praying I wouldn't hear: "Please advise the sergeant that this is a confirmed homicide."

The acrid smell of my smoking brakes assailed my nostrils as I roared into the familiar cul-de-sac and saw the combined lights of three police cars bathing the buildings, the cars, and the curious bystanders with the flashing colors of tragedy. I leapt out of my car and shoved my way through the crowd to where a patrol officer was stringing yellow crime scene tape around the apartment.

"The woman is dead in the bedroom. Looks like they beat her with a bottle," he told me in a quiet voice.

"How about the kids? There was a little boy and a little girl."

He pointed at a neighboring apartment.

"They're in there. The other guys are in there with them. The little girl is okay, I think. But the boy . . . He must have tried to protect the woman. It's a bad one, Sarge. Real bad."

As I strode to the door of the neighboring apartment, another officer came running out to meet the arriving fire department ambulance. When he motioned to the paramedics who were scrambling out of their rig, I noticed that his hands were stained with blood. I stepped past him, through the doorway, careful to avoid the blood trail that snaked along the worn gray carpeting in the living room. I was filled with dread as I made my way toward the kitchen, where I heard voices, but I stopped when I saw Carmelita with a middle-aged couple in the rear patio. The little girl was kneeling, clutching at the hem of her dress, sobbing uncontrollably while the woman tried in vain to soothe her. The man turned toward me for just a moment, and something like an accusation flashed in his eyes.

I stopped in the kitchen doorway. An officer was leaning over, his broad back obscuring my view, but I could see José's thin legs dangling from the kitchen chair, a puddle of blood blossoming beneath him, more blood smeared across the colorless linoleum by the officers' heavy boots.

"You're gonna be okay," I heard the officer say as I stepped around him.

José was sitting rigid in the chair, his eyes glazed with shock, blood oozing down his cheek. The officer was holding a dish towel around the blade of a knife that was jammed into the top of his head, imbedded deep into his brain. I recognized the red handle of the knife. It was the same knife that had been used to slice a piece of cake for me a few hours earlier. I crouched down next to José and took hold of his hand as the paramedics came in and took over for the officer holding the towel. I looked into those unfocused eyes and saw, miraculously, recognition in them.

"You were very brave, José," I told him. "Very brave."

His lips started to flutter. I leaned closer, my ear near his mouth.

"I tried," he whispered. "I'm the man of the house."

Then the paramedics pushed me aside. I walked back out, heat flushing my face. *Those were my words to José,* I thought, *and now they've come back to haunt both of us.*

At Maria's apartment, the officer who had been taping off the scene was now taking notes while talking in Spanish to an elderly man. He glanced up as I approached.

"This is Mr. Sanchez. He lives in the next apartment over." The old man nodded, and the officer continued. "He heard screaming and commotion in the apartment. When he looked out of his window, he saw three Latin males running past. He opened his door to see which way they went. That's when he heard them."

"Heard them?" I asked, and looked over at Mr. Sanchez. He took a step closer, and what he said brought the reality of cruelty once again into sharp and bitter focus.

"It was laughter," he told me in a voice suffused with disbelief. "They were laughing as they ran away."

I turned away and walked slowly, almost on autopilot, back into Maria's apartment. I stopped in the kitchen and looked down at the floor where the once neatly sliced birthday cake lay crushed amid smashed dishes and scattered utensils. I walked down the hallway where Carmelita had run earlier. The silence was nearly deafening; the house was deathly quiet. I stopped at the first of the three open bedroom doors; I smelled death before I saw it. Maria lay face up across the rumpled bed. The crushing blows from the forty-ounce beer bottle had made her face unrecognizable, and I felt the same rage build inside of me that I have tried to control since the first time I saw the horrors humans can inflict upon one another so many years ago.

The rage deflated into a sense of helplessness in an instant when I caught sight of something familiar on the gory bedspread. It was my official business card, the embossed golden badge floating impotently in the congealing mass of Maria's blood.

DOMESTIC

PERHAPS IT'S A FEW STRAY NOTES OF A SONG PLAYING ON THE radio or the glimpse of a young woman when she tosses her hair a certain way that dredges up a forgotten memory. Some such memories are pleasant, some are painful—nostalgia no matter how sweet is always tinged ever so slightly with regret. Today, on this idle sunny afternoon, it was the acrid smell of spent cordite wafting across the currents of a gentle spring breeze that triggered it—unbidden and largely, I had thought, forgotten.

It's so strange, I mused. How we act at the time an incident occurs, how we are perceived by those around us, doesn't necessarily reveal what we feel or how much. That's training; that's survival instinct. That's the job. It's like radiation poisoning—exposure to the mirthless and merciless banality of evil and indifference. You don't know you've got a fatal dose until your blood feels thin and you stumble over words and objects in your path. Then, when you are most vulnerable, some image comes out of nowhere and hammers you.

"You here for qualification?" The stentorian voice of the rangemaster, a lean and grizzled Vietnam vet, snapped me back to the here and now. I looked around me, blinking. I was midway across the newly mown grass, literally midstride, as if I were in a state of suspended animation. My cracked but gleaming gun belt was draped over my shoulder; my patrol car was parked behind me, the only one in the lot on this weekday afternoon.

"Yeah," I said, and started for the row of empty wooden bleachers that serves as seating for the various police marksmanship competitions. I set my gun belt down and took a deep breath, inhaling the rich chlorophyll smell of the fresh grass. The rangemaster watched me quizzically for a few moments, but since I wasn't offering any explanation, he wasn't asking.

I leaned my hip against the weathered green wood of the bleachers and gazed at the cloudless azure sky enveloping the mountains surrounding the Las Vegas valley. The rangemaster went back to what he was doing: silhouette target practice at thirty yards with a matte black .45. Once again the smell of cordite assailed my nostrils. I saw then that I wasn't alone; a young cop, eager and agitated, was trying to catch my eye. He was standing in the middle of the pistol range, between the rangemaster and his target, oblivious to the danger he should have been in. For a long moment I refused to look at him and instead savored the austere but dazzling view. I have learned over the years, though, that when ghosts want to visit on the waves of memory, it's best to invite them in. I sat down on the bleachers and patted the seat beside me and let the ghost prevail.

Suddenly we were standing on a rain-slick sidewalk in a middle-class residential neighborhood on the Westside a few days before Christmas. It was freezing, and my slicker wasn't keeping the rain from running down the back of my neck and under my collar. The young cop was waving pages of notes from his patrol officer's notepad under my nose, expecting me to be as overwrought as he was. I looked down: Bic blue-ink jottings in a forceful but cramped hand, almost illegible.

"Why don't you just tell me, Langdon?"

"Langford. Sir."

"Just tell it to me, Langford. Take a deep breath."

"Sergeant—"

"Pretend you're telling me a story, Langford."

Dawn and Karen had been shopping early that afternoon, he said. Even though it was the Friday before Christmas, they had braved the local shopping mall. Despite the hassle of trying to find a place to park and the long lines in the department stores, they had enjoyed themselves. They were both sixteen years old, just a few months apart, stepsisters but closer than many sisters linked by blood. Dawn was dark and petite, and Karen was lanky and blonde, both pretty and exuding a small-town friendliness that hadn't faded in the three months they'd lived in Las Vegas. They made friends easily, even in new environments, and were well on their way to being "popular," something they never aspired to but enjoyed nonetheless.

"Does this have a point, Langford?" I asked, to hurry things along. I was watching as the detective's unmarked sedan pulled in behind the paramedics' bus. Another officer was stepping over puddles on the lawn as he strung crime scene tape around the house. Langford followed my gaze and then swallowed, his Adam's apple bobbing in his throat, as he tried to find his place in his notes.

They're getting younger and younger, I thought. *What is this kid, twenty-two?* He was fresh out of the academy—five weeks, maybe—where he'd spent six months being stretched to the limit physically and emotionally. There was no other way to find out who could not only do the job but could survive it. As his FTO, his field training officer, my job was to push him even harder and to watch, to note, and to evaluate every move he made. He was a rookie cop—we called them "trainees"—and not all of them made it. I couldn't tell yet whether this one would. I had to turn up the heat a bit and see what this kid was made of. Just that morning, while walking to the patrol car, my shotgun resting casually against my shoulder while he lugged everything else we could possibly need, he told me that he'd graduated from college just last year. He'd majored in religious studies, wanted to be either a minister or a cop. *Ah, that's great,* I thought. *A hand-holder.* Most of the new kids made up for their lack of experience and worldliness by packing a little extra bravado in their words or a little inflated authority in their deeds, but this one was going to subdue the savage beasts with compassion. *Great,* I thought. *Just great.*

Dawn's father, a carpenter, had been divorced when he met Karen's mother, a title clerk in an insurance office, five years ago in Portland, Oregon. She had been divorced as well and trying to make it on her own with her eleven-year-old daughter. That was the first thing they had talked about, the fact that they were both raising young daughters alone. The two girls had become instant best friends.

The move to Las Vegas was the blended family's new start. In a city where the population boom meant more than a thousand new homes a month, there were plenty of job opportunities for a skilled carpenter, and an insurance title clerk could work anywhere. The girls looked at it as an adventure and were delighted to live where the sun shone all the time. Many of the kids at school were "new kids," so fitting in was not a problem. Karen's mom found a good job almost immediately, and though Dawn's dad was still looking for "the right opportunity for someone of his expertise," they knew it was just a matter of time until he accepted one of the many offers he had received. All in all, they were a very happy family.

I looked closely at Langford. There was no irony in his voice, no cynical arch to his sandy eyebrows. "Why don't you come and take a look," I said, starting up the walkway to the house.

Langford stayed rooted to the spot. "I'm just telling you what I have in my notes, Sarge." He held them up again for me to see. "This is what I have in my notes. Look."

Before I could reply I had to move aside so that the coroner's crew could roll their stretcher up the walkway to the covered front porch and wait out the rain while the investigators did their thing inside.

"Afternoon, Sarge," one of the technicians said, grinning at me. I knew him; he was a biker in his off-hours, a Harley man with a skull shaved as smooth as a cue ball, never without a cinnamon-flavored toothpick in the corner of his mouth.

"What's up, Harley?"

"I fucking hate it when it rains."

"Tell me about it."

He laughed and I laughed and Langford just stood there like

a bird dog, pointing to his notes as if there were some truth there. I almost felt sorry for him.

"All right, Langford. But get to the point."

Dawn and Karen had stopped at a nearby fast food restaurant on the way home from the mall and had bought a couple of tacos to hold them over until dinner. Both had their driver's licenses and were allowed to take Karen's mom's car out provided it was daylight and they only went locally. They were in a hurry now, though, not because it was getting dark but because they were hoping to get home before Dawn's dad got back from picking up Karen's mom at work. The girls had purchased presents for their parents—a scarf for her and a tie for him—and they wanted to hide the gifts in their closet until they had a chance to wrap them.

Karen was driving. When they pulled into the driveway they noted with dismay that their father's Ford Bronco was already there, the engine ticking from its recent drive. Karen particularly noticed that the Bronco still bore its Oregon license plates. She wondered why Dawn's dad hadn't gone down to the DMV to get those changed to Nevada plates. *Until that last thing gets done,* she thought, *it's like we're only here temporarily.* And it was starting to rain.

"I'll sneak the presents in the house," said Karen.

Dawn nodded, giggling conspiratorially, and replied, "Okay. I'm going to run next door and show these to Nina. I swear I'll be right back." She held up the pair of costume jewelry earrings she'd purchased at JCPenney, and Karen smiled and nodded her assent.

Karen walked up the driveway, pulling her sweater tight around her slender frame. She headed around to the back of the house because she knew the back door would be unlocked. She hadn't even reached the door when she heard the TV. It was so loud. *That's odd,* she thought. Her mother and stepfather never watched TV in the afternoon; they rarely switched it on until it was time for the six o'clock news. Karen shut the door behind her, listening for any sounds of movement as she tiptoed across the kitchen floor. Suddenly she had an embarrassing thought. What if they had turned on the TV to mask the sound of lovemaking? Karen knew that Nina's mother and father did that sometimes, though they weren't fooling anyone. Karen and Dawn had speculated about their parents' sex life, of course, but Karen didn't recall ever seeing so much as a caress between them. They were always so very polite with each other, almost formal. They weren't expecting the girls for another hour or so, though. What if they'd taken advantage of their children's absence to enjoy each other intimately?

Karen stifled a giggle. She just couldn't picture her mom slipping into something sexy from Victoria's Secret. She couldn't picture Dawn's dad offering anything more than a perfunctory peck on the cheek. But you never knew.

"Mom? Dad? I hope you're decent!" she called out cheerily as she started down the hall to the bedrooms. Maybe it wasn't nice to interrupt, but she had to pass their bedroom to get to hers, and their door was wide open.

That was the detail that tweaked some alarm in the back of her brain. Her mom would never do *anything* with the door open, of that she was certain.

"Mom? Dad? Are you alright?"

Langford and I had just finished giving a ticket to a tattooed lowrider whose bass was booming so loud that car alarms went off as he cruised residential streets.

"You don't just wait for calls," I told him as we got back into the patrol car. "You look for things. You want to be proactive." *Ah, hell,* I thought, *it's starting to rain.*

"All units in the Union area, report of a woman screaming in the front yard of 124 Bingham Avenue. Nothing further at this time."

Langford stiffened. He looked at me questioningly.

"Go ahead and answer. Don't forget to give our location," I advised. He reached tentatively for the mike.

"Control, 3-Union-34, en route from West Command area." His voice had jumped up a couple of octaves. Adrenaline does funny things to the human voice, and it takes a couple of years of being on the job to be able to control it enough to avoid instantaneous "adrenal dump."

"We're right around the corner from Bingham," I told him, but before I could offer anything else the dispatcher's voice burst out of the radio.

"All units en route to 124 Bingham, only additional is that there are two women screaming something about blood over and over. The caller is a neighbor."

"Tell her we're arriving," I directed Langford as I scanned the houses for numbers through the swish of the windshield wipers on the patrol car. But it was the screams that directed me to the house.

Two young women were standing at the end of a driveway near a newer black Ford Bronco with Oregon plates. The taller one was blonde. She was young, maybe mid- to late teens, and her face was blank with shock. She was holding a smaller girl with dark hair tightly to her chest, keeping her from breaking free while stroking her back to comfort her. The dark one was crying in gulping, convulsive sobs. The blonde was whispering, "Sssshh . . . sssshh . . . ssshh . . ." It was a third girl, about the same age as the first two, who was standing in the driveway of the house next door and screaming.

"Blood! Oh, my God, there's blood everywhere!"

I glanced over at Langford as we pulled to the curb; his eyes were as big as saucers, and his hand was hovering near his service pistol. I knew this could be anything, and I didn't want Langford stumbling into something he wasn't prepared for. As we got out of the patrol car I ordered him to watch the house and to get the girls out of the way and stay with them and find out what happened.

"Who's inside?" I asked the screaming girl.

She shook her head vehemently and screamed, "No one! They're dead! They're dead! Oh, God!"

I saw the blonde girl wince; I heard the dark one in her arms moan like an injured animal.

"Ssssshhhh . . . Dawn . . . Ssssshhh . . ."

Langford, shaken but determined to be a cop, pulled out his notebook and Bic pen and hustled the girls into the neighbor's yard.

"Can one of you tell me what happened?" I heard him ask.

I still didn't know what the hell was going on. I drew my pistol as I approached the wide open front door. With my other hand, I reached for my portable radio.

"Control, 3-Union-34. Request backup, officer entering."

As I went in the front door, I peeled to the right with my pistol held in a combat grip and extended in front of me. I quickly surveyed the Sears-functional living room. Nobody was there, but the television was on and annoyingly loud. I crossed to it and switched it off. Then, as if one sense had been masking another, I smelled the faint smoky odor of gunfire. And the metallic stench of blood.

I moved slowly down the hall, my heartbeat reverberating in my chest and my ears. The first bedroom—clearly a teenage girl's—was empty. They were in the second bedroom, the master bedroom.

The woman was blonde, the same hair color as the girl standing in the front of the house, though hers had faded with age, maybe with neglect. She was seated against the wall next to the bed. She had no right eye. The .357 Magnum slug had left a huge gaping hole where the eye had once rested in her skull. Pieces of bone and gray chunks of brain splashed with blood decorated the wall above her like some macabre modern art canvas: Jackson Pollock gone homicidal. Incredibly, she still had her reading glasses perched on her nose, and though the lenses had been blown out, the frames were intact. She was in her forties, I imagined, dressed for work in a dark skirt with a royal blue turtleneck sweater. Her legs were chunky in her nylon stockings, her ankles swollen.

My eyes traveled across the room to where he sat on the floor next to the window. I assumed they were man and wife because they wore matching gold wedding bands, both now splattered with blood. I holstered my pistol. His temple had borne the contact shot, and blood hung in strands from his nose and mouth to the floor. The exit wound had taken out half his head, leaving the precise color of his thinning dark hair a topic for conjecture. He had been thin and wiry, with a weak chin and a downturned mouth. He seemed to be frowning at the big revolver that lay in his right hand, anchoring it to the floor.

A domestic, I thought. *A fucking big finale to a usually pedestrian call.*

I heard sirens approaching, and I made my way through the rest of the house to make sure there were no more surprises before I walked back out the front door. I stood on the porch and watched the ambulances arrive and watched the rain come down. Langford, I saw, was on the porch next door, talking to the two girls—one blonde, one dark—and taking notes. They were seated in a porch swing now, a blanket around their shoulders. He looked up at me questioningly; I shook my head.

Twenty minutes later we were standing together on the sidewalk in the rain and he was reading me his notes. His interminable notes.

"What does all that have to do with anything, Langford?" I asked, pissed off at the senseless tragedy inside that house.

"Dawn's father killed Karen's mother, Sarge."

"Then himself. I got that. So what?"

He shook his head and looked over to where the two girls were being helped into the paramedics' bus. "It's just that Karen— she's the blonde girl—she's trying to protect Dawn, the other girl, from what happened. Karen wouldn't let Dawn look. But it was Karen's mother who was murdered by the other girl's father. Do you see what I'm saying, Sarge?"

"The other girl will find out eventually, Langford. It's not going to stay a secret."

"I know, but that's not what—"

"Go in and take a look," I ordered. "You're going to have to get used to it."

I swear I thought I was doing him a favor and doing my job as his FTO. The kid had never seen a dead body before, much less a violent murder/suicide. This was part of the job, and it was better he dealt with it now, with me there, than when he was out on his own and alone. He stared at me for a desperate minute and then squared his shoulders and headed inside. I followed him so that I could see how he reacted. The coroner's investigator was inside with one of our homicide detectives. They were both taking notes; the bodies were still exactly as I had found them, still leaking. The stench of cordite was still heavy in the air. Langford stood for a long time in the doorway of the bedroom—no one noticed him—and he tried to absorb everything. I have to admit, he tried. He gulped a few times and asked a dumb question or two before he turned a serious shade of green. Then he bolted past me, tumbling against the hallway walls as he ran. He ended up losing what remained of his lunch on the rain-soaked lawn.

Harley grinned. "Get used to it, kid." He turned to me, shifting his toothpick from one side of his mouth to the other. "Been a long time, hasn't it, Sarge?" He didn't mean since the last time we were at the scene of a double homicide. He meant since the last time we reacted the way this kid Langford had done. Harley and I could leave the scene that minute and go have a pizza and a beer. We could talk about our favorite football team or about office politics without giving another thought to what we'd just seen.

"Maybe too long," I said, looking at Langford bent over on the lawn. I watched him wiping his mouth with the back of his hand.

Now, seated on the bleachers at the pistol range, I watched Langford, the trainee, the ghost, walk away with a long-forgotten memory that had somehow slipped into my consciousness along with the smell of cordite on a gentle breeze. Langford is not dead; in fact, after that domestic call he was the best trainee I ever had. He went on to be a top street cop, and he's now a sergeant over at Northwest Station. I took credit for training him as well as I did; I take full responsibility for that. But something happened that rainy December afternoon, and I was witness to it. That's the substance of the ghost that I'm watching walk stiffly across the range even as the rangemaster reloads and fires again.

When we drove away in the patrol car that day in the rain, I saw their eyes meet, Langford's and Karen's. She was looking out the window of the ambulance; Langford was looking out the window of the patrol car. They shared something. I think now that they had both been witnesses to the death of innocence. In each other. When her stepfather took her mother's life and then his own, he murdered the innocence in the two girls. There weren't just two victims in that murder/suicide, there were four. And when I sent Langford back into that house, his trainee's innocence was lost. That was his job, after all. That's what we do. We swear an oath, and an aspect of duty is seeing, constantly, what no one should ever see. I knew that then; I know that now. But it doesn't always help. Like today.

"Thanks," I called to the rangemaster.

"You're not going to shoot?"

"I don't think so. Not today."

I drove back to work.

HONOR THY MOTHER

THE MOTHER. The mists of time surrounded Doris Bentley as she lay motionless in her narrow bed. The small room was painted in comforting pastels—pale yellow, blushing pink—and the framed lithograph prints on the wall depicted apple orchards and rose gardens and weeping willows on a riverbank. It was pleasant and quiet, an effective disguise for what this place really was, a hospice for the dying. This was where the last days of the terminally ill were made tolerable with regular and increasing doses of mercy-morphine, where tearful family members came to say their good-byes, or sometimes ask for forgiveness.

Doris had been there for three weeks, drifting in and out of consciousness and abandoning lucidity for a kind of painless oblivion when the voracious appetite of the cancer gnawing through her life made the pain unbearable. There were moments when she would awaken and her papery eyelids, alabaster and blue-veined, would flutter open and she would look around for Emily. Her little girl, Emily. When she was awake she would look out her tiny window onto the grassy verge and daydream. She would indulge in pleasant memories of her only child, the skinny girl with the lopsided grin and a long blonde braid running down her back who loved hot dogs and macaroni and cheese and playing Scrabble on the porch on summer evenings. It had been hard when Charlie died; she had to go to work, and the only job she could find was cleaning hotel rooms downtown. But it had been worth it; whenever she came home exhausted and despairing, she'd pull up outside her apartment in her old Rambler station wagon, and Emily would fly toward her and fling her arms around her neck.

"I'm so glad you're home, Mommy!"

THE NURSE. Diana Ames wondered at the smile on Doris Bentley's face. She would often see it when she came in to check the vitals on her patient, and she wondered what the old woman was thinking about that managed to lift her from her haze of pain. Diana had been a nurse for a long time, and she knew that every patient who came to the hospice had to face death in the same manner in which he or she had lived. Some with fear, some with sadness, some with hope. It was the individual parade of memories that marched through every patient's subconscious as he or she lay hooked up to an IV, breathing shallowly, that defined what each would feel at the end. *She's reliving her happiness*, thought Nurse Ames as she patted Doris's hand. *She must have had beautiful things in her life.* That was good, too, since she knew Doris would be lucky to make her sixty-fifth birthday next month; her cancer had progressed so far that there was little anyone could do but try to make her comfortable at the end.

"Emily?" came a faint voice from the bed. It was so weak that Nurse Ames was not even sure that she had heard it.

"No, Doris, it's your nurse, Diana. Is there anything I can get for you?"

Emily, she wondered. *Who's that?*

THE COP. My workweek was almost over. In just three hours I was going to park my patrol car in its slot at the station, toss my uniform into my locker, and head to the airport. I was going to be catching the red-eye from Las Vegas to New Jersey to visit my parents and to escape the oppressive desert heat. A cocktail or two in flight was just what the doctor ordered, and I intended to be a good patient.

I rolled down the window in my air-conditioned vehicle just to feel the blast of dry heat and to savor what I would soon be leaving behind. I was tired. It had been a long few months with nothing out of the ordinary happening on the streets, just all the petty and often bloody squabbles that had become almost generic in their regularity. He said, she said. He told me to empty out the cash register. She tried to run her over with her car. It's not my drugs; I never saw it before. Why'd I run?—You scared me, sir. I didn't do nothing. She hit me first. I didn't see the kid, I swear. We were just having a little talk, that's all—I don't know how she got that bruise. He's bleeding?—Ah fuck, it wasn't me! Two drinks, that's all I had, Officer. Hey, Officer . . . Officer . . . Officer.

During the twenty years I'd spent as a cop, ten with sergeant stripes on my arm, there's little of life's urban turbulence I haven't seen or heard or haven't pretended to understand. But life has a way of working you over—like a prizefighter on a heavy bag—when you least expect it.

"614, Control," the dispatcher intoned over the radio. I yanked the mike out of its bracket and answered, hoping she wasn't going to burden me with anything that would interfere with my heading in a bit early to get my paperwork done. I intended to catch a quick beer on the way to the airport.

"Control, 614, go ahead."

"614, Control. Unit 3-David-21 is responding to a domestic violence call at Desert Hospice. He's requested that you be notified."

Hospices aren't exactly a hotbed of police activity, so my curiosity was piqued. I checked out the details on my mobile computer. There wasn't much there: "Hospice nurse reports an elderly female patient has been beaten by an unknown woman. Ambulance is en route to transport to medical center trauma unit." That was it. Who would attack an elderly woman in hospice care? Another patient? It didn't make sense. *The dying,* I thought, *should be off-limits to the rages of the living.*

As I drove to the hospice, I thought about my own parents three thousand miles away in New Jersey. I was flying out to visit them because they were no longer able to come to see me. My mother, who was in her early seventies, had slipped last year and broken her hip. She was still confined to her bed, and the doctor had recently indicated that she might not be able to travel again for some time, maybe ever. Every year, for all the years I had lived in Las Vegas, they had flown out from New Jersey during the winter months to escape the bitter Northeast cold and to visit me. Now it was up to me to fly to see them, which is why I had a plane ticket in my pocket for the red-eye flight. This call—so vague on the computer monitor—sent a chill down my spine, and reflexively I vowed that neither one of my parents would end up either in a hospice or alone. Then I arrived.

I pulled into one of the EMERGENCY VEHICLE ONLY parking spots, which were discreetly positioned out of the public's view. Another unit was already parked there, but the ambulance had not yet arrived. *Jesus*, I thought. *To wind up in a hospice only to be yanked out and dumped into a trauma center. Is there no pity in this whole damn world?* Then I saw another officer, a seasoned cop with two hash marks on his sleeve, coming through the automatic glass doors.

"Hi, Sarge," he greeted me. His name was Gino, if I remembered right.

"What's up?" I asked.

"Some sick shit," he said, then turned to look at the slender, dark-haired nurse stepping outside and coming toward us. She was about forty with kind eyes and a sad, tremulous smile. "This is Diana Ames. She's the nurse here. Better you hear it from her."

"Ma'am." I looked at her expectantly. Behind the sadness, I saw fury in her eyes.

"The woman who was hurt is my patient. Her name is Doris Bentley. She's sixty-five years old and has incurable stomach cancer. It metastasized . . . she's dying. She doesn't have more than a few weeks at best."

"How long has she been here?"

"Less than a month. Not long. She is a very sweet, very dear woman."

"What happened tonight?"

"I was doing charts . . . I was the only one on the floor. Margo had run over to admin to get some cups. Visiting hours had just ended. We didn't have many visitors tonight, so that's why I noticed her. She was walking back toward Mrs. Bentley's room, but I didn't actually see her go in—"

"*Who* was walking toward Mrs. Bentley's room?"

"I don't know who she was. I'd never seen her before."

"Then what happened?"

A few minutes later, as I turned down the hall toward the victim's room, I thought about what the nurse had told me. A large woman, obese and tall with stringy peroxided blonde hair, had lumbered down the hallway to the patients' rooms. She was wearing green sweatpants, scuffed tennis shoes, and an oversized gray bowling shirt with ROSCO'S emblazoned on the back. The nurse had not seen her face. Presumably she had gone into Doris Bentley's room, and in a matter of minutes the nurse could hear yelling coming from down the hall. She thought Mr. Fitzsimmons had turned up the volume on his television again—this was practically a nightly occurrence—and she was just about to leave her desk to talk to him when the yelling stopped and the big woman stomped toward the glass doors.

"You didn't know her?" I'd asked.

"I'd never seen her before, I'm sure. I would have remembered someone like that."

Watching the woman's departure, the nurse felt a tug of alarm and found herself hurrying to Doris Bentley's room. *Just as I was doing now,* I mused, and pushed open the door.

A staff doctor was bent over the figure in the bed. It was a hospital bed, I noted; but for that and the intravenous rack attached to one side panel, the room could have been excised from any midrange hotel in the city. Brass floor lamps cast a soft glow over the cozy surroundings. Cheerful, subdued, no individuality whatsoever. No cards, no flowers, no personal items, I noted. I wondered whether she was completely alone in the world. Then the doctor backed away from the bed. Even in his physician's coat with a stethoscope around his neck, he looked all of seventeen with his wire-rim glasses and acne scars. He acknowledged me without speaking; his mouth was set in a grim line as he nodded at the wraithlike figure on the bed. I stepped closer and got my first look at Doris Bentley.

She was lying on her back, emaciated by prolonged sickness and ineffective cures. Her breathing was ragged. But it wasn't the manifestation of her illness that was so disturbing. Blood oozed from a cut on her forehead; the delicate blue surface veins fed the thin stream that dripped down the bridge of her bony nose, leaking onto her cheek and into her mouth. The bedcovers had been pulled back to reveal her blood-spattered yellow nightgown. I felt myself wincing inside, though nothing showed on my face. I stepped closer. Her skeletal arms were nearly translucent, and I could see the IV needle clearly under her skin. Several patches of flesh had been ripped away on her hands and arms, exposing the raw meat that lay beneath. Someone had beaten her.

"How is she?" I asked the doctor.

"She was helpless." An angry flush shot up his neck, and I noticed his lower lip was trembling. Then I felt it, too—a rage so white-hot that it seemed to burn my flesh from the inside; I hadn't thought I was capable of feeling this way anymore. Cruelty and crime, victims and suspects: The dance of violence had been a part of my life for so long that I thought I was inured to the senseless pain people could inflict on one another. But this frail little woman, living out her last wretched days in a sterile hospice room, moved me in a way that I have no words to describe. I only knew that she deserved her dignity, her moments of peace, but whoever had brutally beaten her had robbed her of that. This crime was beyond the statutes of law; it was a moral crime. For the first time in my long career as a cop, I wanted retribution. And I wanted to inflict it.

"Sergeant?"

I turned and looked at the middle-aged man in a rumpled suit who was standing hesitantly in the doorway. I stepped outside the room, wanting to shield her indignity from the rest of the world.

"Jack Williams," he said, extending his hand. "I'm the administrator here." I shook it even though I didn't like the way he was frowning and making a *ttsskk, ttsskk, ttsskk* sound. "This is bad business . . . bad business." I wondered if he meant that literally.

"I need information on her family, her next of kin," I told him.

"Mrs. Bentley had no visitors during her stay with us."

"She did tonight."

He looked at me then, a smile playing on his lips as he wondered if I was making a joke. I wasn't. I didn't move, but he saw something in my eyes and shuddered involuntarily. Then he was all business. "Of course, of course. Come with me. I'll have one of the girls get you the information you need."

While I copied down the addresses and telephone numbers of the meager contacts in Doris Bentley's file, the paramedics arrived and crowded into her room with a stretcher. A few minutes later they were wheeling her out, hooked up to all the lifesaving gadgets they had in their gear bag. It made her look even smaller and frailer than she was. The senior member of the crew caught my eye and motioned me over. Doris Bentley's eyes were open, and she was looking around in confusion, in fear.

"They had her on morphine for the pain. It's wearing off. That's why she's awake," he said, taking me aside.

"So now she's in pain."

"Pain like we don't want to know about."

"Then fucking do something for her."

"Wish I could . . . Listen, Sarge, I don't think she's going to survive. We'll get her down to trauma, but . . ."

I knew what he meant. Anything she said now could be crucial to the prosecution. This might be my only chance to find out what happened.

"Let me ask her a couple of questions," I told him.

"Make it quick, Sarge."

I approached the gurney and wrapped my hands around the rails as I bent down close to her. I caught a whiff of the metallic odor of blood and the sharp aroma of stale urine and something else that reminded me of damp earth. *Dying,* I thought, *is like being partially submerged in your grave while still alive.*

"Hi, Doris . . . Mrs. Bentley. My name is Randy. I'm with the police department. Can you tell me what happened tonight?"

Her eyes rolled back in her head and then darted from side to side like a frightened animal's. A thin moan seemed to come from inside her chest; her mouth didn't move. I gripped the rail even tighter and was about to repeat my question when I felt her icy fingers weakly grip my wrist.

"She's a good girl. A good girl. She loves me."

"Who, Doris?"

"She didn't do this."

Then I knew. Even in her dying and deplorable condition, she was protecting someone. I put one of my hands over hers and gently squeezed.

"I know she does," I said softly. "But sometimes people who love us do things to hurt us without meaning to. They don't want to. They just can't help it." My lies were soothing and encouraging, but inside my anger raged.

I saw the hesitation in her rheumy eyes as she searched my face to see if I was sincere, if I really understood. I leaned closer and whispered in her ear.

"Is that what happened, Doris?"

Her fading eyes locked on mine, and she nodded.

"Sometimes she gets mad. She doesn't mean to hurt me." The tears that had pooled in the corners of her eyes spilled over and ran down her mottled, bloodstained face. "She doesn't know how to say good-bye."

"Blood pressure's dropping!" shouted one of the paramedics.

"That's enough!" said the senior crew member. "We've got to go!"

I ran beside them as they went out the double glass doors.

"Who, Doris? Just tell me who." But her eyes had already closed.

Gino came outside and stood next to me. He had his pad of notes in his hand. We watched the ambulance drive away, watched it until it disappeared.

"You get anything out of her?"

"Nothing," I said. "Nothing at all." I told him to make sure that the homicide detectives were on their way and to notify the crime scene folks. This was going to turn out to be a murder. Then I started for my patrol car.

"I'll be back later," I told him.

I saw the surprise in his eyes; he wanted to ask where I was going, but the row of hash marks on my sleeve kept him from saying anything.

"Sure, Sarge," I heard him say as I drove off.

I was four blocks away before I pulled over and unclenched my fist and looked at the slip of notepaper in my hand. There hadn't been much to copy down in Doris Bentley's file. There was just her next of kin, the person to contact in case of an emergency. Her daughter, Emily.

The apartment complex was on the east end of the city, squat and squalid and situated under pale pumpkin-colored sodium lights. Oil spots on the concrete carport looked like bloodstains, but maybe that was my frame of mind. I pulled the patrol car to the curb and wondered what I was doing. I'd just walked out on a crime scene where I was the primary; I was way out of my sector and off the radio. *Just turn around,* I told myself, *and get out of here.* But I didn't. All those years I spent stuffing my emotions back into my gut, cutting off the blood supply to my soul, had finally risen to the surface like bile. These feelings, this state of mind, I knew, were more dangerous to a cop than a bullet. I got out of the car.

I found the manager's office, which doubled as his apartment, and after repeatedly knocking with the tail end of my flashlight, I heard a gruff voice from behind the door.

"All right, goddamn it, all right."

The door swung open, and a chubby and grimy troll of a man in a stained undershirt and boxer shorts looked out at me from behind the security screen. I was immediately enveloped in a pungent cloud of marijuana smoke. The troll gaped and was instantly obsequiousness in full display.

"Oh, hi there, Officer. What can I do for you?"

"I need the passkey to apartment nineteen in building six," I said without preamble.

"Is there a problem, Officer?"

I sniffed the air pointedly. "There can be if I don't get that passkey."

He blinked a few times and then nodded rapidly and tottered back into his apartment. He kept the master keys on a corkboard next to a giant freshwater aquarium. He rustled around there for a minute, the vibrantly colored fish watching his every move.

"There," he muttered, and returned to the door holding a key in his hand. It was attached to a white cardboard tag and was marked "6-19."

"Is there a problem, Officer?" he repeated as he opened the security door and handed me the key.

"I'll let you know," I said.

Apartment 19 was on the ground floor. There were no lights on, but before I knocked on the door I listened for the sound of a radio or television, anything to indicate that someone was inside. There was nothing.

"Metro Police," I said loudly to the closed door. There was no movement, no sound. None of the neighbors had looked out, either. I only hesitated a moment before I slipped the key into the lock and opened the door. I unholstered my .45 and spoke again, this time to an empty room.

"Police. Anybody home?"

Doing a room search for a suspect, any suspect, is not a one-man job. *Add this,* I thought, *to the list of procedures and laws I've broken tonight.* It wasn't reason that was fueling me but some primal force that I couldn't even identify, much less control. I stepped inside and shut the door behind me.

I went quickly from room to room, my gun drawn, making sure that no one was in the apartment, using only the ambient sodium light that leaked in from the street. When I was satisfied that I was alone, I holstered my gun and used my penlight to explore the musty apartment. Food-encrusted dishes filled the sink, and empty whiskey bottles were piled atop empty beer cans in the overflowing trash can. The odor of rotting garbage permeated the apartment, but there was also the stench of bodily decay—what I'd smelled at the hospice.

I found Doris Bentley's bedroom. The room was crowded with furniture that was too big for the small space, but it was neat and clean, as if her house-proud nature had been shunted to this tiny corner while chaos took over everywhere else. The only evidence of disruption was her unmade bed; I could see the empty plastic bags on the floor where the paramedics had tossed them in their haste as they struggled to start an IV line. *Nothing,* I thought, *has been touched in here for nearly a month.* There was a pillow pushed against the wall. I picked it up and turned it over. Somebody had stitched, in a very careful hand, HONOR THY MOTHER amid a border of hearts and flowers. I saw a photograph next to the bed and picked it up to look at it more closely. I recognized a younger, more vital Doris Bentley; her eyes hadn't changed. She had her arms around a young girl who was maybe eleven or so; the child's bright blonde hair was pulled back into a long braid. Both mother and daughter were smiling for the camera; the girl's grin was engaging, lopsided. Doris was radiant. *This must be the daughter, Emily,* I thought.

"What the fuck," I said out loud to nobody, or maybe to a past that had no obvious link to the garbage-scented future I was standing in. Then I heard the muffled ringing of my cell phone on my belt.

"Sergeant Sutton."

"Sarge? This is Gino."

When I didn't respond, he said, "I got some news from the hospital."

"How's it looking?"

"The old lady didn't make it, Sarge. She's dead."

I was expecting that, but I felt my limbs go numb and heard a buzzing in the back of my skull.

"Be sure you give everything you've got to homicide," I told him while thinking that the needle was too good for the callous bitch who had beaten an old woman to death. Life without possibility of parole, that would be more like it. Thirty years of something to think about while shuffling around Nevada State Prison in shapeless gray prison garb.

"Homicide isn't responding."

I thought I hadn't heard him right. "What? What do you mean they're not responding? This is a murder, isn't it?"

"The district attorney said there's no way he could prosecute since she was dying already. He wants us to treat it as elder abuse. If we can get a suspect, that is. What d'you think? One of the nurses maybe? . . . Hey, Sarge . . . where are you?"

I was speechless. *Elder abuse,* I thought. *A two-to-six felony.* I could see the district attorney avoiding the cost of a trial by taking a plea and offering probation and anger-management counseling. *Oh, yeah,* I thought, *that would do a lot of good since the object of the anger was dead.* I pictured my own mother imprisoned in a hospital bed after brittle bones betrayed her. I pictured myself standing by helplessly in the shadows, willing to do anything but really only able to try to make her comfortable, and love her, while she healed. Maybe this was what brought the horrible reality of Doris Bentley's despicable death to a sickening crescendo.

"I'm just getting some coffee," I said, and hung up.

THE DAUGHTER. I sat in the living room, in the dark, on the edge of a lumpy couch with my .45 in my lap. I didn't have to wait very long before I heard a key scratching in the lock. The door swung open, the light switched on, and she was standing there, weaving slightly on her feet. I could smell the alcohol from where I sat. A large woman, obese and tall with stringy peroxided blonde hair, wearing green sweatpants, scuffed tennis shoes, and an oversized gray bowling shirt with ROSCO'S emblazoned on the back. Now, however, she was holding a bowling trophy loosely in her chubby fingers. She smiled when she saw me; the lopsided grin had turned malevolent with age and hard living.

"What the fuck do you want?" she said.

"Where's your mother, Emily?"

"Why the fuck should you care?"

"What did you argue about today?"

She gave me a kiss-my-ass look, set the trophy down on the carpet, and started toward the kitchen. In an instant I was across the room, one hand gripping a handful of her hair, the other holding the muzzle of my Glock just inches from her face.

"Where's your mother, Emily?"

"For all I care, the bitch is dead."

She didn't get the last syllable out of her mouth before I back-handed her across the face. She pitched backward and fell onto one knee next to the counter that separated the kitchen from the dining/living room. White heat roared up the sides of my face, and I found my arm raised with my pistol poised to slam down on her head. Then I spotted the serrated-edge bread knife lying on the counter just a few feet from the woman wiping blood from her mouth.

She glared at me with raw hatred. "Who the fuck do you think you are to come in here and—"

It's how it looks sometimes, not how it actually plays out. I knew there wasn't a jury in the world that would convict me given who I was and given what she had done earlier in the evening. So I reached out and grabbed the knife and tossed it to Doris Bentley's only child. It was a reflexive action; she reached out and caught it without even thinking about what she was doing. I saw it then—the hint of fear in her eyes.

"Where's your mother, Emily?" I asked.

EPILOGUE. When I got back to the hospice, the crime lab was there, and two of the crime scene investigators were bagging the bloody sheets from Doris Bentley's bed. The dark-haired nurse was sitting in the nurse's station, her eyes red-rimmed from crying. I found Gino—he was questioning the last of the on-duty staff—and handed him a cup of coffee. I took a sip of mine.

"Thanks, Sarge," he said as he pried off the plastic lid. "You didn't have to go out to get this, you know. There's a fresh pot in the lounge."

"Yeah, well, fuck it."

He looked at me curiously, then looked down at his notes.

"The next of kin is a daughter named Emily Stuart. She lives off Eastern and Charleston. Want to run over there?"

I shook my head. "The detectives can handle it. Let's just call it a night"

If I said I didn't remember what happened after I threw that knife, I don't think it would sound like I was telling the truth. But I honestly don't remember. I made my flight to New Jersey; I sat beside my mother for a good part of the next day basking in the warmth of her presence and willing her to heal. When I got back to work, everything was like it always was, and life, and the job, continued.

Maybe there are some things you're better off not knowing, but they always come back to haunt you until you feel compelled to tell someone. Anyone. Maybe you just write it all down—and then wait and see what happens.

MY CHILD

THE UNMISTAKABLE HERALDS OF AUTUMN—THE SCENT OF fallen
leaves, the first chill in an evening breeze, the high-pitched giggles
of the barely-teenagers back at school after the long summer—
swirled through the open window of my patrol car, bringing forth
images of my earlier life. The flaming brightness of the foliage
that surrounded picturesque New England villages flashed
through my mind: The burnished leaves of the trees—riotous in
scarlet and crimson and pumpkin orange—had made it look as if
the landscape were ablaze. Three Bridges, Little York, Brass Cas-
tle—towns that I would drive through late at night, my windows
rolled down, in my quest for peace and some respite from loneliness.

That was long ago and more than three thousand miles away.
Nearly twenty years ago I'd left my hometown police force and
come to Las Vegas, lured like almost everyone else by the glossy
and glittery advertisements spewed forth by the chamber of com-
merce, which promised twenty-four-hour excitement, the neon
bulwark against aloneness. Now, pushing a black-and-white
through the backstreets of the tourist mecca of the world, I looked

out at the litter-strewn pavement, the hulks of abandoned cars bathed in the pale luminescence of the few streetlights that had survived the nightly target practice of bored gangbangers, and wondered about how we all end up where we do. These neighborhoods bore no resemblance to that promise of the better life; the people who live in these crowded apartment gulags seem to have been stripped, just like those abandoned cars, of everything including their dignity.

I'm still driving alone at night, I reflected; *only the landscape has changed.* I struggled to shake myself out of this nostalgia for a season and a place that no longer existed for me.

This is what I was thinking as I cruised through a public housing apartment complex. I had another two hours to go on my 3:00 P.M. to 1:00 A.M. shift, and there wasn't much happening on this Sunday night: It was quiet, and a lull like this is dangerous for a cop. I had to fight to keep my edge until shift's end; surrendering to this autumn lassitude could get me killed.

My headlights caught a white Ford Bronco just up ahead. It was stopped in the middle of the street, sitting at a severe angle to the curb. I flashed my high beams and caught the images of a number of people running away, disappearing into the darkness. They looked like cockroaches fleeing across the linoleum when the kitchen light goes on. The odd sight sent adrenaline surging through my system, and my heartbeat kicked up a couple of notches. I reflexively reached for the microphone resting at the side of my radio. All senses now on full alert, I scanned the area up ahead for possible threats, and as I cruised slowly to a stop, I brought the mike up to my lips to advise dispatch of my location.

I had just pressed the transmit button when a woman stumbled out of the darkness, running toward me from my left. She was young, early twenties maybe, plump and plain-looking though now her features were distorted with fear. I didn't know what to expect; she was white, and I rarely saw white folks in this neighborhood. Maybe she was so obviously panic-stricken because her car had broken down in an area she was unfamiliar with.

Before I could reply to dispatch, the woman was at my patrol car window, breathless, spittle flying as she leaned in and screamed, "He's up there! He's up there!" She pointed at a two-story fourplex unit just up the street.

"Unit transmitting, state your call sign." The woman's screams must have gone out over the air when I had the transmit button depressed.

"614, Control, hailed by a citizen, unknown trouble, Simmons south of Carey," I radioed, then tossed the mike onto the seat. I quickly got out of my unit. Unknown trouble means your patrol car can wind up as your coffin if you get caught sitting in it at the wrong time. Since I had no idea what was going on here, I wanted out.

"Whoa, slow down," I said to her. She was whimpering, barefoot, jumping from foot to foot as if the pavement were still hot from the afternoon sun. "Who's up there?" I asked in my practiced firm-and-in-control voice.

"The boy!" she shouted at me, her eyes accusatory, as if I should know what the hell I was there for.

She grabbed at me, trying to pull my arm, and I disentangled her fingers quickly and held her back so that I could look right in her eyes.

"Ma'am, you're going to have to tell me what's going on. What boy?"

Tears erupted from her eyes, and mascara slid down her face and dripped off her chin and onto her dirty T-shirt.

"The boy who got hit by the car!"

Then I could see people stepping forward, out of the shadows, black folks with concern etched on their faces. A toothless man with his gums the color of an old eraser, his ebony face shining with perspiration, nodded vigorously and pointed at the fourplex up the street.

"Like she say. Up there."

I grabbed for the portable radio on my gun belt and called in.

"Control, 614, roll medical for an injured child, auto accident victim!" I turned to the young woman and the old man and demanded, "Which apartment?"

They both answered at the same time, talking over each other. "Up there! That one! See? 202!"

I took the crumbling cement steps two at a time as I rushed toward the open door at the top of the landing. Weak yellow light spilled out, and in the shadows I could see a child's bicycle lying on its side. The combined wailing of several women—a siren song from the heart of bedlam—met me as I pushed my way into the small apartment. There must have been eight women crushed in the living/dining room, at least three generations of African American women, all kin, all terrified. Their voices had the resonance of the Mississippi Delta; their eyes were wounded with centuries of suffering that I could never begin to comprehend. It was like a maelstrom inside that room, a swirling mass of colorful fabric, of keening women in pain. The scent of lilac mingled with the scent of fear.

"Where is he?" I shouted, and almost supernaturally the women stepped back and stood motionless, eyeing me with such naked hope that I felt my knees weaken. I saw him. He was maybe six or seven years old and was lying on his back on a tattered couch, his eyes open, seemingly staring up at the ceiling, one arm flopped unmoving toward the bare floor. There was no blood, no visible wound other than a tiny abrasion on his chin; I thought his injuries must be internal. I knelt down beside him and touched the side of his neck with my index and middle fingers, searching his warm skin for some sign of a pulse, but I felt nothing at all.

"How long has he been like this?" I turned and shouted to the women. One elderly, heavyset woman shook her head, tears dripping down her cheeks and splashing onto the floor.

"Just a minute, just a minute, no more, no."

I grabbed him off the couch and laid him down on the hard floor, scattering the panicking roaches, and got down on my knees, tilting his head back. I placed my fingers over his nose, placed my mouth over his, and gave him three quick breaths. His lips were warm against mine, and as I withdrew my face from his and placed the palms of my hands over his thin chest, I searched his expressionless eyes for some sign of life. There was none. As I yelled for the women to clear the room and for someone to go downstairs and direct the paramedics up to the apartment, I began compressions.

It is during times like these that we all find ourselves making deals with God, or the Devil, or whoever might be listening out there, whoever might hold sway over life and death. As I alternated between chest compressions and forcing my own breath into his lungs, I willed with every fiber of my being that he should live. Each time I brought my mouth to his, I looked into his dull, lifeless eyes and tried to force my life's vitality into his small body. Over and over, again and again—it was just that young boy and me, beating back some specter of mortality. Sweat ran down my arms, pooled around my fingers, soaking his shirt and giving him evidence of life he could not create on his own.

I don't know when I became aware of it, but I think I heard it first—a chanting, a melodious chanting in an unfathomable ancient language. I looked up and saw them then, all the women of this young boy's family: They were kneeling, holding hands, encircling the two of us. They were praying as one, swaying as if buffeted by a terrible wind, praying to some God I would never understand, and then I realized they were praying for me, too, for me to be able to help the boy. Praying for his life; praying that I would have the strength to save him. For a moment, the tiny living room disappeared and I was kneeling over the boy like a priest at a sacrificial altar, bestowing mercy and banishing death, far away in time and place where tall grasses swayed in the moonlight in the rhythm of the chanting women. It was in this surreal moment, as I bent to touch his lips again with mine, that I understood this matriarchal family's fear and grief. He was the beloved princeling, heir to all their love, embodiment of all their hopes, of all the hopes of his ancestors. He was their precious child. And so as I continued, I prayed, too.

It seemed like hours, but it was only minutes, when I became aware of the siren of the approaching fire department paramedics. I felt someone take my hands away and push me to the side, and I watched as a young paramedic placed a stethoscope to the boy's chest. He listened, then turned to me.

"I've got a pulse!" he said. "Good job!"

Everything happened very quickly after that. The paramedics seemed to scoop him up, wrap him in a blanket, secure him to a gurney, and load him into the waiting ambulance in seconds. I don't remember going down to the street, but there I was, watching as they slammed the ambulance doors. Did I bring him back? Or did I just want to so badly that I imagined I had? This was why I wore a badge, I realized. It wasn't for the authority, for the power over people; it was for the chance to save a single life, like that little boy's.

As I ran back to my patrol car to follow the ambulance to the trauma center, I looked back toward the apartment building, but all the women were gone, on their way to the hospital, too, I surmised. All the way there, with the careening ambulance in sight up ahead, I still felt the boy's warm lips on mine and the exultant rush from the paramedic's pronouncement. My shirt was soaked through with sweat, and I could hear my heart pounding in my chest even over the wail of the sirens. I pictured the teddy bear I would bring him later and the expression on his face when he gazed up into my eyes from his hospital bed. *My child,* I thought. *You're my child. I've given you life, haven't I? And from now on, like a father, I will always care for you.*

When I reached the hospital emergency room bay, the paramedics were already pulling the gurney out of their rig and rushing through the sliding glass doors. I followed, intent on the welfare of my child. My only child. He was swept into the curtained sterility and harsh lights, surrounded by masked figures of the trauma team, all in white smocks and blue scrubs. Tubes were inserted into his small body, into his arms, down his throat. Monitors were hooked up with practiced precision, and wires were everywhere. I knew my part was over, but I couldn't leave. I blended into the background, waiting for the chance to see him, waiting for the women in his family to arrive. I watched the weary faces of the off-duty medical staff who lingered near the observation window, their eyes full of hope that this one would beat the odds. I found myself wondering, as I watched, if the boy knew I was there. If he felt the bond between us as I did.

I wandered to the front entrance and found the gift shop. Amazingly, it was still open. An elderly woman with hair the tint of lavender smiled up from her seat at the cash register as I paid for the teddy bear. It was soft and had eyes so wide with innocence that it almost looked real. I went back to the emergency room and stood at the observation window, waiting, a hopeful smile playing on my lips, the teddy bear in my arms.

The boy's heart beat for an hour before it faltered and stopped. I saw the trauma team as they filed out of the room, their heads down in defeat, leaving the boy in there alone—a tiny, lifeless body on a metal table. *He looks,* I thought, *like he's sleeping.* I stood there for a long time, holding back the tears that stung my eyes. Now and then a nurse would pass and touch my arm softly in consolation. Finally they covered his face with a sheet, and I turned away, afraid of the emotion that threatened to consume me.

I drove back to the apartment building. Someone had to tell his family. When I got there, the old black man and the young white woman were sitting together on the curb, watching the traffic cops writing their reports of the accident, using the hoods of their squad cars as desktops. The neighbors were there, too, and on the sidewalk was a makeshift shrine—a burning candle and some bunches of flowers. Everyone looked up at me when I approached, eyes full of expectation, but one look at my face and they knew. The young woman burst into tears, hugged her knees, and rocked back and forth.

I realized then that I was carrying the teddy bear.

"Where are the women from his family?" I asked. "Back in the apartment?"

The old man looked at me. "What women? Nobody up there. His mama still hasn't come home from work. We're waiting here to tell her."

I nodded and set the teddy bear down on the sidewalk, next to the candle, and left them there to their vigil.

"Did the kid make it, Sarge?" I heard the young patrolman's voice before I saw him.

"No. He didn't."

"Ah, man." His face fell. "That's too bad." He looked at me, his forehead creased with worry. "You okay, Sarge? You didn't know the kid, did you?"

"No, I didn't know him." I walked back to my patrol car, into the autumn night, feeling a sudden icy wind blow across my face. Once again alone.

Even now I don't know what happened that night—there is too much I can't explain—but I still feel the loss of that child . . . my child.

THE HONOR STUDENT

THE STREETS CONSUME YOU LIKE A MALIGNANT TUMOR. THEY burn a pathway through your breast until they storm the citadel and lay waste to your heart and the protective layer of innocence and emotion that covers your very soul. You inadvertently become a participant in or a first-row observer to every malevolent act known to man. Murder becomes more than a word or a deed; it becomes an assault on the senses once you smell the stench of its evil and touch the filth of its pain. Rape is incomprehensible until you experience the hollow-eyed stares of the victims. Even the word "victim" loses its impact when you realize that all this label really does is mask the true and dire consequences of flaying open someone's soul to the viscous infection of crime. Eventually "empathy" and "compassion" are merely empty words and the memory of them dims, even extinguishes. Those afflicted wish in vain for the opportunity to be healthy again while knowing full well that neither you, nor they, nor "all the king's horses and all the king's men," as the nursery rhyme goes, could ever put any of you back together again.

This is how I began my memo to the captain. He had asked me to write about the symptoms of burnout, a product of police work and something most cops are familiar with. I'd been a cop for almost twenty-five years and have certainly seen more than a few of my coworkers and friends self-destruct. I could recognize the well-traveled road to hell, and I wasn't surprised when he asked me to write something up. I was surprised, however, when he called me into his office and shut the door and asked me if there was something I wanted to talk about. My memo was in front of him on his desk, and he tapped it absently as he searched my face for something he wasn't finding.

"Why did you ask for this assignment?" he asked me, gesturing around his office to take in the headquarters building, where we were safely ensconced way up on the fifth floor.

"It was a good deal, Captain. Good hours, better pay, a lot of perks. Hell, everybody wanted it."

"Yeah, well, I'm asking about you."

We went round and round and no matter what I said I never seemed to give him the answer he was looking for, so after a while I stood up, looked at my watch, and told him I had a meeting at eleven o'clock.

"When you have a real answer for me," he said, "come back and we'll talk."

Later that afternoon as I sat in my unmarked patrol car in our underground parking lot, I thought about what I hadn't told the captain. I had sought refuge in the administrative job, not an opportunity. I needed to get off the street; I needed a fresh perspective. Pushing paper around a government-issue desk might not boil the adrenaline soup I'd lived on for so many years, but looking into the mirror at my haunted eyes framed by deepening crow's feet told me that it was time to quit facing the dragon. For the first time in my life I felt that the beast—fire-breathing, cloven-hoofed, scale-covered, and visible only in my mind's eye—was close to winning. A lot of things had brought me here, I knew, but they all had culminated in a call I responded to a couple of months before I asked for a transfer into admin. I thought of that call then, as I do now, as my fated encounter with "the Honor Student."

It had been lunchtime on some nothing-special any-day-of-the-week, and my biggest decision of the day was going to be whether I wanted to get my mouth around a loaded pastrami sandwich with brown mustard oozing through the rye or whether I wanted to succumb to a healthy chicken Caesar from Jacob's Famous Deli, the chow hole of choice near Police Central Command. Flying a desk for the second week of my two-week rotation with the Community Services Bureau, I was reminded again of why I never wanted to be an indoor cop who kept his handgun in the bottom drawer of a desk. Lunchtime gave me the opportunity to commandeer a patrol car and go back out onto the streets, even if it was just to cruise the few blocks to the deli.

I rolled down the window and let the cool fall air ruffle my short, graying hair. I didn't bother to log in, so I wasn't being officially monitored by the dispatch center, but I kept the radio on the usual patrol channel so that I could listen—maybe enviously—to the routine chatter of car stops and call reports. I was looking forward to being back out there next week, though at that moment visions of pastrami sandwiches were dancing through my head.

Suddenly the tone alert blared out over the radio signifying an urgent call or crime in progress. Even before the last note faded away, the dispatcher's voice cut in over the air.

"All units in the area of 1425 Gable Street, report of a boy asphyxiating, possible suicide attempt. Any unit that can respond, advise."

My hunger pangs were forgotten. I'd worked that beat for years and knew that Gable Street was just a couple of blocks away. Okay, while I was riding the desk, it wasn't my responsibility to answer calls, but maybe my proximity meant that I could get there in time.

"Control, 614 Admin en route, ETA two minutes."

There was a hesitation on the part of the dispatcher. She'd probably never heard an administrative sergeant respond to a call before.

"Copy that, 614." As I tore around the corner onto Gable Street, I heard a patrol unit radio that he was close to the scene, and as I pulled up in front of 1425, his unit was also arriving. We both bailed out of our cars, our overhead lights almost completely invisible in the blazing Las Vegas sunlight, and I had to steady myself as I fought for balance in an afternoon that seemed to be pulsing with heat waves visibly rising up from the pavement.

"*Hijo! Hijo!*" I heard a man screaming in Spanish, and then a wail that tore straight through my heart.

"Sergeant! Over here!" the young cop called as he vaulted the five-foot cinder-block wall in one fluid motion. I started to follow but then saw the gate and jerked up the latch and barreled through.

The backyard was mostly cement, with a sagging aboveground swimming pool half full of stagnant water. It was next to an early 1960s Chevy up on blocks with its hood propped open and engine missing. A toddler's trike lay on its side. A makeshift clothesline extended from the detached garage to the back porch, and it was filled with men's whites: T-shirts, underwear, and athletic socks. The smell of laundry bleach filled my nostrils as I ran, and somewhere a pit bull barked without seeming to take a breath.

The most undeniable assault to the senses was the sound of the man screaming in Spanish. His words had become unintelligible; all that remained was the lilting cadence of his native tongue yoked to some sound of anguish that wasn't quite human. The open door to the detached garage was the source of the commotion. As I rounded the corner, the uniformed back of the young cop disappeared into its yawning darkness. I followed into a place that was cool and dim. In a strange way the quiet garage reminded me of the interior of a small chapel. It was oddly quiet, and all the sounds, including the screaming man and the barking dog, seemed to stop. It would have been peaceful but for what was before me.

He was a dark-haired boy of maybe fourteen, olive-skinned so probably of Hispanic descent. His hair was neatly cut and combed; he wore starched black pants and a pale blue button-down shirt with a private-school crest on the pocket. A speaker wire wrapped around his neck and suspended him from a low rafter. His face was swollen and purplish. What I remember most clearly is that his knees almost touched the floor, as if he were a penitent kneeling in supplication, though his hands were not clasped in prayer but dangled loosely by his sides.

"Hold him up!" I screamed to the young officer as I yanked out an illegal switchblade I kept in my pocket, confiscated from some gang punk years ago. I sawed through the wire just above the boy's head as the officer struggled to hold him aloft. The wire snapped, and the boy collapsed like a marionette. Both of us lowered him to the floor. Screaming began again in earnest, and people were streaming into the cramped garage, but the other cop and I might as well have been all alone with this young boy, still warm to the touch.

I slipped my knife between the wire and the boy's neck and snapped it. He seemed to exhale and then sink down into himself.

His eyes were open and his capillaries had burst in his retinas, making it seem as if he had been crying and his eyes were red with grief.

"Sarge, I've never done this before!" pleaded the young cop.

"You know how to do compressions, right?" I asked. He nodded, his eyes still wide with panic. He knelt down next to me. "Okay, you just count them—one one thousand, two one thousand, three one thousand—and I'll do the rest, okay? Wait until after I start breathing. It will be after each third count."

I tilted the boy's head back and then in a desperate kiss sealed my lips over his and breathed air into his lungs. The young cop gave it all he had, pushing onto the boy's chest and counting off the rhythm of life; sweat dripped from his forehead, creased in concentration, and spotted the boy's neatly ironed school shirt. I felt the boy's cooling lips on mine, my eyes only inches from his red-rimmed ones, trying to convince myself that I'd misread the signs of death. Perhaps he would suddenly gasp and take in lungfuls of sweet fresh air. Instead, he involuntarily vomited into my mouth, causing me to retch and sit back. Then I saw them: Everyone in the garage, all the boy's family members and neighbors, had moved into a circle around us and were watching us, many with their hands clasped in prayer.

"Please, please, *señor policía,* please save my *hijo,* my son," said the boy's father, his weather-beaten face making him look years older than he was.

"Sarge," whispered the young cop with tears in his eyes. "Is he gone?"

I wiped away the vomit from the boy's mouth and chin and bent down again to try to breathe life into the flaccid lungs.

"One one thousand . . . two one thousand . . . three one thousand . . . ," intoned the young cop like a last-hope mantra.

That's when it happened. I opened my eyes to look at the boy's face and saw instead the face of Patrolman Johnny Rogerson as he lay on his back on the muddy locker room floor nearly thirty years before. I felt dizzy and strange, so I closed my eyes and inhaled again, only to have the sharp odor of pool chlorine suddenly sting my nostrils . . . I felt the damp spot on the front of my uniform shirt where an infant's limp body had lain against my chest as I held her downy head in my hands . . . but I couldn't seem to get enough air to fill my own lungs, much less another's lungs . . . I fought the sense of rising panic and leaned down to breathe again into the boy's slack mouth . . . but it was another boy, a much younger one, who had been hit by a car one summer's night and lay as still as death on a couch in a second-floor apartment so long ago . . . and I felt a sob erupt in the back of my throat . . . and I tasted the blood of the infant Jackie as I leaned over to breathe life into a face that had been shattered by a gangbanger's bullet . . . my fingers scooped away the damaged tissue that threatened to choke her to death as I filled her tiny lungs . . . and then I was spinning back through time and there were more . . . dozens of faces I had caressed like a lover or a parent, trying to breathe life and hope into lungs that had stilled. I tasted all their lips, their sadness, their fear again as I bent over the still form of this young boy who had chosen to hang himself this terrible afternoon. There were just too many of them, too many lungs for me to fill, and I felt myself losing consciousness as I took another ragged breath.

"Randy! Let him go!" The voice was familiar, and the hands that pulled me to my feet were like steel hooks. I found myself looking into the eyes of a lieutenant I'd worked with before. "Let the medics get to him." He looked at me closely, too closely, as if he could see what I had seen. "You okay?"

Instantly my game face was back in place, and I nodded impassively as I wiped the residue of the boy's vomit on the hash marks on my sleeve. "Had to give it my best, L. T. That's the kid's father over there." We both looked over at the figure of a man who had collapsed in on himself. He was trying to slip between the paramedics as they unfurled their high-tech gear and life support gadgets and ripped open the boy's shirt, buttons flying everywhere.

"Stand back, sir," instructed one of the paramedic crew members, but he seemed to melt onto his son's body, wrapping his child in a lonely embrace. We watched as the young cop who had come with me into the garage gathered him into his arms and pulled him away. Maybe it was just my imagination, but I thought they were both looking at me as if I'd failed them.

"Randy?" said the lieutenant, still watching me curiously. "I'll take care of the scene and the father. Why don't you go and question the people in the house. Find out what happened."

Maybe it was stepping back into the blazing sunlight that spurred me to action. Suddenly I was striding across the backyard, ascending the rear porch steps, and crossing through a spotless kitchen. I was met in the doorway to the living room by another young cop, one with maybe two or three years on the job.

"Sarge, from what I can tell, the parents are divorced. The mother lives here with the boy—"

"What's the boy's name?" I interrupted.

He flipped a page in his notebook. "Luis, Luis Mendez. He's . . . I mean, he was fourteen years old and a student at St. Vincent's School for Gifted Children." He looked at me, uncertain whether that fact was ironic, but I ignored the question in his eyes.

"Go on."

"Well, even though the mom and dad are divorced, the dad comes over to take care of the kids when the mom works late."

"Kids?"

"There's an older sister who's nineteen. She's in the living room. She goes to community college and also helps to take care of the younger sister." He looked up at me again, oddly uncomfortable.

"Go on."

"The younger one is disabled. She's in a wheelchair. She's in there, too."

I pushed past him and headed into the living room, which was also spotless, and encountered a sobbing young woman sitting on a floral-slipcovered couch. The room was redolent of air freshener and furniture polish. She held the hand of a horribly disfigured quadriplegic girl of about twelve, whose permanently grinning face was punctuated by frantically darting eyes. The younger girl looked from the figures of the cops crowded into her sanctuary to her sister's grief-stricken profile, trying to make sense of what was going on around her. I couldn't seem to stop staring. Drool hung in strings from her mouth to a stainless steel hospital dish shaped like a half moon on her lap. She made simian grunting noises as she rocked back and forth, her withered arms Velcroed to her wheelchair.

"Angela loves Luis," said the older girl. "She knows when school is over, and she waits for him . . . he feeds her . . . she won't eat for anyone else."

I didn't know what to say. "I'm so sorry about your brother," I said lamely. "Do you know what might have caused him to be depressed?"

"Luis is an honor student. He worked very hard to overcome what happened."

"What happened?" I asked quietly.

"It wasn't his fault," she said, shaking her head adamantly. "Luis was six, Angela was four. It was an accident. It wasn't his fault, and no one blamed him. Not Poppy or Mommy. Not Angela. Angela loves Luis. She won't eat for anyone else." She stroked her sister's hand.

"Lu-u-u-u-u-u-u-u-sssss," gargled the younger girl, strings of spittle flying from her damp lips.

"Luis is an honor student," continued the older sister. "He only wants to make his family proud." She choked on a sob. "He wants to make up for . . . for what happened, but he doesn't need to. He's such a good boy. An honor student. Always getting the best grades . . . but that doesn't matter to Angela. She will only eat for Luis." And she looked at me with eyes wide with fear. "Oh, God, now what will we do?"

"Show me what happened *today*," I said. Some hint of understanding was prickling my consciousness.

She looked at me for a moment, then nodded. She gently let her sister's hand go and got up. Then she led me toward the hallway. I followed, but I glanced back at the little girl in the wheelchair. She went on keening and rocking, trying to free herself from her Velcro restraints, while all the cops looked helplessly at each other.

"Lu-u-u-u-u-u-u-u-sssss . . . Lu-u-u-u-u-u-u-u-sssss" followed us down the hall to a tiny back bedroom. It was decorated with St. Vincent's school pennants and framed certificates of scholastic achievements. Everywhere I looked was the name of Luis Mendez, honor student.

Like the rest of the house, the room was spotless. Only the purple and black nylon bookbag, which had been thrown carelessly across the bedspread of the single bed, was out of place.

"Is Luis dead?" she asked in a whisper.

Her big eyes were brimming with tears, but in them I could see that glint of irrational hope I had seen too many times.

"He's gone to the hospital with the paramedics" was all I could offer. "Now show me. Please."

It was there, the reason. It was in the guise of a crumpled piece of paper lying just under the hem of the bedspread. I picked it up and smoothed it out in my hand and took it over to the window where I could read it better. Luis Mendez didn't make the honor roll this time.

"Lu-u-u-u-u-u-u-sssss," came the hardly human wail from the front room.

"It didn't matter," the older girl sobbed. "It didn't matter to any of us!" She ran blindly from the room.

It must have mattered to Luis, I thought, looking down at the paper in my hand. I felt as if I had been hit from behind by too many lost lives. I reached up and rubbed my lips where they had been bruised during the failed kiss of life. I heard something breaking inside of me.

The streets consume you like a malignant tumor. They burn a pathway through your breast until they storm the citadel and lay waste to your heart and the protective layer of innocence and emotion that covers your very soul.

The captain once again had my memo on police-officer burnout in front of him. "Are you sure there's nothing you're willing to talk to me about?" he asked.

I thought about the Honor Student and all those who had preceded him, but I shook my head NO. "There's nothing, Captain." I looked at him and he looked at me, and though we shared a lifetime of such experiences we never acknowledged them or our inseverable connection to each other. Maybe that was the greatest loss of all.

"Let me know when you finish your report," he said, with something like grief momentarily clouding his features.

I went back into my office and retrieved my gun from the bottom drawer. I wasn't planning, I realized, to go to lunch.

You inadvertently become a participant in or a first-row observer to every malevolent act known to man. Murder becomes more than a word or a deed; it becomes an assault on the senses once you smell the stench of its evil and touch the filth of its pain. Rape is incomprehensible until you experience the hollow-eyed stares of the victims. Even the word "victim" loses its impact when you realize that all this label really does is mask the true and dire consequences of flaying open someone's soul to the viscous infection of crime. Eventually "empathy" and "compassion" are merely empty words and the memory of them dims, even extinguishes. Those afflicted wish in vain for the opportunity to be healthy again while knowing full well that neither you, nor they, nor "all the king's horses and all the king's men," as the nursery rhyme goes, could ever put any of you back together again.

DEATH DANCE

"MY NAME IS RANDY SUTTON, AND I'M A COP. I'VE BEEN WEAR-ing a badge for almost thirty years, and although I don't consider myself a tough guy, you don't survive for that long by not being able to take care of business. I work the streets of Las Vegas, and no matter what you think you know about the glitzy Strip, it's a city that can be cold even in the sweltering August heat."

That's how I almost began my story, and though it's true, maybe I am avoiding "the issue," as the department shrink says. I've been ordered to go twice a month, but I don't have much to say. She says I should "write down" my thoughts, but I don't know, I think work is the cure, and I've been putting in a lot of overtime lately. You see, late last year my partner and best friend was shot to death in the hot wax compartment of a Westside car wash where he'd chased and cornered an ATM robbery suspect. I was half a block away at the time, cuffing the second suspect, a crack addict with a runny nose. But I've dealt with it. What could I have done differently?

Earlier this afternoon I was out alone in my sergeant's squad car when I started rolling toward a call at a convenience store, even though it wasn't in my beat. The first officer on the scene, a young and inexperienced cop with about two years total on the job including his time in the academy, radioed to dispatch that he had arrived. Moments later I heard his voice jump about three octaves.

"Control, 3-Baker-24, get me a backup! Suspect armed and has a hostage!"

I floored the accelerator and flipped the toggle switch that activated my light bar, and my siren pierced the stifling air with its urgent wail. I was on the scene in seconds and spotted the distinctive tail of the first patrol car peeking out from the far side of the convenience store. Robertson, the young cop, was crouched behind his black-and-white, using the trunk for cover. He had his semiautomatic pistol aimed beyond my point of observation. He was in combat position, the tension of the situation evident in his stance. I pulled my patrol car up behind him and saw that his pistol was pointed at a small red compact parked next to the side of the building.

"Throw the gun out—Now! . . . I said now!" Robertson was shouting textbook commands at the passenger side of the car, his voice quavering like an adolescent's.

I grabbed my twelve-gauge pump gun as I rolled out of my patrol car, and, using the front of my car for cover, I took my position and yanked the slide, jacking a load of double-ought buckshot into the chamber. The metallic *snick-snick* sound of a twelve-gauge being primed is unmistakable and a serious attention-getter. I finally got a good look at what was going on in that red compact. The man in the passenger side—late twenties or early thirties, military buzz cut—had one sinewy hand wrapped around the arm of the driver, a terrified-looking young woman in her late teens or early twenties, while the other was holding a small revolver next to her skull. He was tapping her with it gently just above her right ear as if imitating some percussive beat that only he could hear. Then, as if he could feel my eyes boring into the back of his skull, he turned around in his seat and looked right at me and grinned.

He wasn't as old as I had thought: twenty-five at most, with a thin face and big ears that flapped forward like Dumbo the Elephant's. It was his eyes that held me, though. They were crazy eyes. Muddy blue and flecked with yellow; focused yet vacant at the same time. The kind you look into and know that something isn't right, was never right. He pulled the terror-stricken girl closer to him and caressed her chalky cheek with the blue steel barrel of the revolver, all the while smiling at me as if we were rivals for her affection. Then he turned away and lowered the gun so that for a moment I couldn't see it, and he leaned over and whispered something in the girl's ear. I could feel her shudder ten yards away, and her body, rigid with fear, began to shake violently. He turned his gaze back to me. Then, strangely, I could smell carnauba wax in the air from a distant car wash. I laid the twelve-gauge over the hood of the patrol car, its gaping maw ready to swallow the grinning man in the red compact.

"Drop the gun out of the fucking window, *now!*" The grinning man got a stricken look on his face; his mouth opened and closed a few times without any sound coming out, like a fish flopping around at the bottom of a boat. Then a high-pitched wail came out of his mouth—oddly feminine and plaintive—and he shouted at me.

"Don't you curse! Don't you dare curse in front of my girl!"

I felt like I was looking at him through the wrong end of a telescope. I couldn't stop looking at his mouth—the grin had twisted into something cruel, his oddly swollen red lips looked rubbery and wet. Two more patrol cars were arriving. The cops were jumping out, drawing their guns, assessing the scene, and taking their positions. I felt the hot metal of the blistered car hood scorching my arm as I moved into a kneeling position; I thought this was going to go on for hours. Then the grinning man surprised us all. In one fluid motion he leapt out of the passenger door and stood facing us, as still as a statue, his hands behind his back. All the cops were now screaming the same refrain.

"Put your hands up!"

"Let me see those hands!"

"Drop the gun, *now!*"

But I said nothing. I simply waited to catch sight of the gun that I knew was in his hand behind his back. The terrified girl scrambled out of the driver's seat, fell onto the pavement, then scrambled up and ran jerkily toward Robertson. In my peripheral vision I saw him grab her by the elbow and pull her down behind cover. I held the pump gun steady, took a good look at him. He was a wiry little monkey of a man with a mat of coarse hair rising up from the neckline of his sweat-soaked lime green T-shirt. He had on stained black jeans with a western belt buckle that said TEXAS. Despite all the yelling, all the weapons aimed at him, the grinning man simply stood there staring. At me.

Then he began to walk toward me, ignoring all the frantic orders to halt, his hands still hidden behind his back. I couldn't take my eyes off that freak-show face, and I felt his strange eyes boring into mine. Hot drops of sweat poured down my forehead, and in that brief moment I knew what he wanted: to die. What had he seen in my eyes? Some perverted kindred spirit, for at that moment I, too, didn't care about my life; I didn't feel anything at all. I slowly rose to my feet as if controlled by the same mad puppeteer, violating every safety rule a cop is taught. I stepped around to the front of the car, leaving its life-prolonging safety, and started to-ward him. There was no other sound at all besides my footsteps. All the other cops had become silent as they witnessed this tableau unfolding before them.

We closed the gap between us, neither of us daring to break eye contact. We were just a few feet away from each other when, as if by mutual consent, we both stopped. The grinning man was wait-ing like a lover, his moist mouth quivering with anticipation . . . as I brought the shotgun butt up and slammed it full force into his jaw. He flew backward, a look of utter surprise and betrayal on his face in that moment when he realized that the sweet oblivion of death would not embrace him. I only remember hitting him once. Then I felt the strong arms of the other cops tearing me away from where he lay crumpled, sobbing, on the ground, the gun still in the car where he had left it. He wasn't grinning anymore.

Then I was back in the sweltering heat of the summer after-noon, and I became uncomfortably aware of the stares of cops and bystanders alike as I walked back to my black-and-white. I threw the shotgun into the trunk and drove off to write this while sitting in my patrol car parked in the back of an abandoned shopping center.

I figure I'll get my car washed and waxed before I go back in and then give this story to the shrink on Tuesday—or, better yet, tear this up and start it like I meant to, since work is the one thing that brings me any peace and I don't want to lose that.

"My name is Randy Sutton, and I'm a cop . . ."

THE 3:00 A.M. PHONE CALL

NO 3:00 A.M. PHONE CALL BRINGS GOOD NEWS. THIS ONE WAS no exception.

After a ten-hour shift pushing a black-and-white in one of the busiest urban hell-holes in Las Vegas, my ass was dragging. I'd gotten off shift at 1:00 A.M., changed out of my uniform in the station locker room, and driven straight home. We'd run call to call all night long, so I found myself pouring a tall cold scotch within minutes of walking through my front door. I knocked it back and crawled into the cool sheets for a solid night's sleep.

The ringing of the telephone somehow dipped into my adrenaline-charged dreams. I don't know how long it rang before I finally surfaced and fumbled for the receiver. My eye blearily caught the digital numbers of the clock just as it flashed 3:00.

"Hello?" I said groggily.

"Hi, Sarge . . . I'm really sorry to wake you up."

I recognized the voice instantly. It belonged to a young cop from my hometown police department. He was going through the hiring process for the Las Vegas PD, and I was guiding him along. He was a real good kid with about three years on the job and all of his enthusiasm and idealism still intact. He'd been in town a few weeks ago, and now he was back on the job in the East Coast hamlet where we'd both grown up.

"What's up, Zach?" I asked.

"I . . . I just needed to talk to somebody."

I sat up, swung my legs over the side of the bed, and rubbed my eyes with the heel of my hand. Whatever it was, I knew it wasn't going to be good.

"Talk to me, Zach."

I could hear his sharp intake of breath and then a long sigh that ended in what sounded like a child's whimper, and I knew that way down at the other end of the line, wherever he was, he was crying.

"It's my partner, Sarge. My partner . . . he's dead."

I was completely awake then, as if I'd just stepped out of a cold shower, and I felt a chill flutter down my back and pool like ice around my kidneys. *A line-of-duty death,* I thought. *Some bastard out on the street murdered him.* I tried to remember Zach's partner's name, but I couldn't; I'd never met him, I only recalled that he had about ten years on the job and that Zach had spoken about him with reverent respect. His partner was someone he wanted to emulate, Zach had told me in so many words, and I remember envying the rookie awe this veteran cop had engendered in Zach.

"How did it happen?" I asked gently.

"I can't believe it . . . I just fucking can't. What the fuck was he thinking?!"

He started to sob.

I sat up straight and switched on the table lamp by the bed. For a terrible moment I wondered if Zach was in some way involved in his death, if there had been some kind of accident.

"Zach? . . . What do you mean? What happened? Were you with him?"

He didn't answer for a long moment; I heard him trying to stifle his raw grief by gulping back his tears.

"I found him, Sarge. I found him."

His voice went flat, void of emotion, as if he were out on patrol and radioing in a report of a dead body to dispatch, using his cop mask to shield himself from something unspeakable.

"I found him in the parking lot. He was in his car. He'd shot himself."

Memories of another time and place seized hold of my senses, and I found myself catapulted into an out-of-body experience. I was standing in front of the small-town city hall that housed the police department—that sheltered the entire city government, for that matter. I had worked there for nearly a decade, and the scene was as familiar to me as my own house. Now I was seeing what Zach must have seen. The streetlamps cast everything in an eerie frosty glow. The scent of magnolia blossoms lay heavy on the summer night's air. There were cars in the parking lot, and the lights were on behind the Venetian blinds in the police department windows on the second floor. I saw Zach pull into the parking lot in his Toyota truck and glance over at his partner's car, not thinking a thing about it as he strode into the building, close to being late.

"He wasn't in roll call, Sarge. That's what struck me right away. I saw his car in the parking lot, but he wasn't inside the building. He never misses roll call, that's just not like him. I waited around for him. I thought maybe he was talking to somebody and he'd be along right away."

From my odd, disembodied perspective from across the street, across the years, I was watching the partner's car, straining my eyes, hoping for signs of life. It was a red Trans Am with a pair of white racing strips that seemed to split the trunk, climb over the hood, and disappear.

"I was thinking about his car out there, Sarge. Thinking maybe he'd fallen asleep or something. I thought I'd better go out to check."

It was the sob that erupted in his voice that brought me back into my bedroom, sitting on the edge of my bed, the telephone receiver gripped so hard that my fingers were numb.

"Take your time, Zach. It's okay."

"Jesus, Sarge, oh, Jesus! He'd put his gun in his mouth! You fucking know what that does to you!"

Yeah, I did. I could picture it. I felt like I was leaning down next to the opaque glass in the driver's window and being struck first by the odd fact that moonlight seemed to be inside the car, streaming from the rooftop like a tiny spotlight onto a tragedian's stage. There's a figure there, a shadowy figure, motionless, slumped over. Maybe he is asleep. It's when you open the car door and the dome light turns on and you see all that blood and there's the smell, too, one you recognize immediately—the iron-and-mold stench of death and the acrid smell of gunpowder—that you know. That hole in the roof, you see then, is quarter-sized and charts the path of the bullet roaring through the roof of the mouth, through the brain, and exiting out the top of the skull and launching itself like a missile toward the full moon.

"I've seen suicides before, Sarge, but I when I saw him, I just didn't know what to do. I froze. I must have stood there staring at him for a full two minutes. It was like a bad dream. I must have thought if I just didn't move I could wake up and none of this would be happening . . . I sound like a fucking idiot, don't I? Ah, Jesus."

I could feel him unraveling; I wanted to keep him talking.

"What did you finally do, Zach?"

"I guess I just went back inside. I remember going up to the sergeant and saying something . . . I don't remember exactly what I said. He made me stay inside while he and a couple of the other guys went out. They found it; I didn't see it. I didn't see anything but him."

"They found what, Zach?"

"The note. They found the note. Jesus, Sarge! Just a couple of days ago we went bowling, for chrissakes! He was fine—I swear to God, he was fine!"

"Do you know what the note said?"

I could hear his ragged intake of breath, and he spoke so softly that I had to strain to hear what he was saying.

"All it said was 'I'm sorry.' That's all, 'I'm sorry.' He didn't say why. Fucking Christ, I don't know why! I was his *partner*—I should have known something was wrong!"

I interrupted him; I knew where he was going with this, and I knew guilt and blame eat away at suicide survivors like battery acid on exposed skin.

"Listen to me, Zach. You had nothing to do with this. There was nothing you could have done. He made a choice. A terrible and selfish choice that was his and his alone to make. Don't take this on yourself—don't let him put this on you."

"Sarge?" His voice suddenly sounded terribly young. "The note . . . the note was addressed to me."

"Ah."

I didn't know what else to say. That maybe he didn't have any-body else to tell? That that's what partners are for? Everything I could think of sounded trite and hurtful.

His voice recovered its timbre, and now he only sounded tired, terribly tired. "Hey, look, Sarge, I don't know why I'm calling you about this out of the blue. I had your number . . . I couldn't think of anybody else . . . Hey, I'll let you go. I'm real sorry about waking you up—"

"You were right to call me. You can call me anytime you need to talk. I wish I had some magic words for you, but none of us knows what's going on in someone else's mind, not even a close friend's, not even a partner's. The investigation may shed some light on what led up to it, but it might not. You have to be prepared for that."

"Sure. Okay. Goodnight."

He hung up. I knew sleep would not come to me again without help, so I got up and poured myself another scotch. I carried it with me out into my backyard, where I leaned against the railing of my gazebo and stood gazing at the clouds. They were swirling languidly across the black sky, irradiated by the light of the full moon. A gentle breeze seemed to caress my face as I replayed the conversation over in my mind. Was there something I could have said that would have helped him? I knew the statistics on police suicide, how ugly the reality was. Twice as many police officers commit suicide as do members of the civilian population. More cops commit suicide than are killed in the line of duty; cops have a life expectancy of eight to twelve years less than anyone else, and the most prominent reason for this is their rate of suicide. Yet no one talks about it. It's a dirty little secret, and if we pretend it doesn't exist, it'll go away.

I know where it comes from; every other cop does, too, even if he won't talk about it. The constant barrage of cruelty, of sadness, that each and every cop is exposed to in his workday life takes a larger toll than any of us are likely to admit. We wear it well, our cop face, impervious, it seems, to the horrors we encounter every day on the streets.

In more than twenty-five years on the job, I've lost friends and coworkers to this insidious beast, and I feel as powerless to help as I did in my rookie years. How do you console someone who shows no outward sign of despair? How do you extend a hand to help someone who never comes close enough so that you can see the nearly invisible sparks of pain that seem to arc like shooting stars in the depths of their pupils? If Zach, sitting beside his partner on four ten-hour shifts a week, couldn't see it, who could? It's like being ambushed; you never see it coming.

As I drained the scotch and poured another, I thought about how suicide diminishes those who are left behind—as if all the moisture, which is life, is sucked right out of them and desiccation sets in. Suicide survivors seem to walk stiffly and are slow to laugh, as if they've been ill and never quite recovered. I thought about Zach's phone call and how inadequate my words were. I didn't convince him not to blame himself; I wondered if I'd helped him at all.

"Selfish asshole," I said to the moon, to the partner with the name I couldn't remember. "How the fuck could you do such a thing to that kid?" Then I felt bad for even thinking that, knowing that feelings of impotency, of inadequacy, bubble to the surface in all of us as anger.

I felt the fatigue and the scotch double-team me, but before I dragged myself off to bed, I went through my house and into my garage. I turned on the light and looked at my collection of things, my "pressure release valves," as I called them—my motorcycle, my jet ski, my gear for rock climbing, for water sports. What I needed most to look at was covered tightly, like my pride and joy or like a demon in a basement—I never know which it is. I unsnapped the car cover and pulled it off and took in the sight of my red Trans Am with the opaque windows, with the two racing stripes that seemed to split the trunk, climb over the hood, and disappear. I had driven it out here from back east, had parked it in the garage of my new house, and had never driven it since.

I opened the door and sat inside, remembering another night in a parking lot adjoining the small-town city hall, sitting in my uniform, my loaded gun in my lap, looking at nothing but the irradiated clouds as they drifted in front of the full moon. That was a long time ago.

I opened the glove box and took out a note that I'd shoved in there years before. "I'm sorry" was all it said, and I recognized my own handwriting. I also knew the sharp metallic taste of a gun barrel in my mouth, but that was my dirty little secret, wasn't it?

When I woke up the next day, my head was pounding, but I almost immediately got back into my routine, into the rhythm of my life on and off the job. For the next week or so I thought about calling Zach, but I thought he'd be busy helping with funeral services and working; besides, I figured that since I had no nuggets of wisdom to share, I'd be likely to let him down anyway. The truth? I didn't want to dredge up memories that I had buried and was not willing to exhume. *That decision, that lie,* I told myself, *has haunted me to this day.*

One morning, several weeks later, I happened to glimpse the postal carrier making his drop-off to the line of mailboxes at the foot of my driveway. I was pouring a cup of coffee, just enjoying the time to myself. I was still on swing shift and tended to view late morning as my leisure time. I sipped my coffee as I sauntered out to retrieve the collection of envelopes and circulars that populated my box. I carried them back inside and made my way to the trash can in the kitchen, idly tossing most of what I held in my hand. There was one plain white envelope that caught my eye. It was handwritten and bore the printed name of my old police department with Zach's name written in ink on the flap.

He's a good kid, I thought. Here he was, in the midst of all his personal anguish, taking the time to thank me for being there for him. As I slipped a paper knife under the sealed flap, I was thinking I should give him a call and see how he was doing. I unfolded the single sheet of paper and felt my legs turn to rubber as a burning heat seared through me, blurring my vision, causing my guts to clench.

"Dear Randy, I'm sorry" was all it said.

WILLY

THE SUMMER HEAT WAS INTENSE, AND THE HUMID AIR CLOAKED me in its floral-scented grasp as I sat on the wooden slats of the bench. My eyes drank in the lethargic movements of the people pulsing along the sidewalks of the downtown shopping district. This was the town in which I had grown up, though I hadn't been back in more than twenty years. I gazed at the storefronts, absently counting how many were still in business from the years when I had walked a foot beat on these streets. Zero. All the old merchants, the mom-and-pop operations, the quirky shops, were gone, replaced by national chain stores and boutiques. Yet the town had retained the stately Colonial facades, and the mature trees lining the wide main street provided a lush green canopy over the pedestrian walkway. Shoppers strolled; no one hurried, and the sweet smell of honeysuckle mingled with that of gourmet coffee and fresh baked croissants.

It was this scent of honeysuckle that brought the memories flooding back, that awakened something that had lain quietly in the back of my consciousness for so many years. Sitting there I could see myself, almost flesh and blood, as I, too, strolled along among the pedestrians. But I was in a city patrolman's uniform, just twenty years old, giving a wave or a nod to the business owners I passed, sneaking appreciative peeks at myself in the polished glass of the storefronts, marveling at the sight of the stiff blue uniform and the silver badge.

I had been raised in the comfortable suburban sprawl of this picturesque town and joined the thirty-five-member police force a couple of years after graduating from high school, fulfilling a goal I'd set for myself in childhood. When I first put on that uniform, and the badge with "Patrolman" engraved over a number assigned to me, I nearly burst with pride.

I came back to the present when the sweat, which had beaded up on my forehead, trickled down behind my ear. I flicked it away like a pesky insect. That's when I heard the rhythmic scratching of the broom on the sidewalk—*swish, swish, swish*—monotonous strokes that for some reason sent a chill up my spine. I turned toward the source, and that's when I saw him. Adrenaline surged through my veins, and I was momentarily deafened by a throbbing sensation as blood pulsed into my brain, but my expression remained impassive behind my dark sunglasses, and I regarded him without evident emotion. I recognized him. His face was in profile and, as gaunt and unshaven as it was, there was no mistaking it. I wanted to get up and walk away quickly before he had the chance to see me, but I forced myself to remain. I took a series of deep breaths as I had done hundreds of times in the past twenty-five years of being a cop. I forced my body to respond as it had been trained, to regain my calm and to remain in control. Through this all I watched his metronomic sweeping of the dirty concrete sidewalk. He held a splintered broom in one hand and a rusted metal dirt collector in the other. His head was cocked at an odd angle and remained stiffly in position as he surveyed the squares of cement, like maps to labyrinthine lands. Each step that he took was awkward and jerky, as if his body wanted to move in two directions at once. Every movement seemed a great effort; each time that he stopped to wipe the sweat from his forehead, his arm had to make its way in a wide circular motion because he could not lift it directly. Every tortured step brought him closer to me, and I saw clearly that, although he was close to me in age, his face was that of a man much older. His cheeks were pinched, his flesh was gray, and the lines around his eyes were deep furrows as if some physical pain had worn away the flesh and bone like a slamming tide. As he limped closer, his broom seeming to draw him forward like a partner in a perverted waltz, my heart began to slam in my chest. He must have sensed me sitting there, for he raised his head and his eyes glossed over me, then darted back as recognition struck him. He froze there, his eyes locked on mine, strange eyes, one drifting to a corner of his upper eyelid, the other plagued by winking tics.

"Hello, Willy" was all I could say.

The spittle on his lips bubbled and his Adam's apple bobbed with anxiety as he finally uttered, "Y-y-y-you."

One word from a face as fixed as a mask, yet the hatred was palpable. I found myself spiraling back in time to a filthy alley six blocks away at 2:30 in the morning more than twenty years ago. I believe he joined me on that journey.

The snow had been falling since shortly after I began my shift at 11:00 P.M. Since one guy was on vacation and another was off sick, we had only two cops and a sergeant working that night, but nothing much ever happened midweek on graveyard shift anyway. At that time, I had been a cop for a year and a half and had lost my gray-area distinctions; I pretty much saw the world in terms of black and white. Striding into the station in my blue uniform after eight hours' sleep, I was eager to hit the road. The sergeant and the other patrolman working that night just grinned and shook their heads at their eager rookie; each had more than twenty years on the job, and they weren't in any hurry to brave the cold to drive around the empty streets looking for trouble that they weren't going to find. Gerry, the sergeant, stopped me before I left for patrol.

"Hit the doors early tonight. Just get the center of town done. I don't want you freezing your ass off rattling doorknobs."

"Yeah, sure, Sarge." I clapped him on the shoulder and headed out the back door to my patrol car. One of the duties of a small-town cop was "walking the doors," a holdover from the earliest days of police work. An officer parks his patrol car near the downtown district and goes on foot through the deserted streets to make sure that there are no signs of breaking and entering in any of the businesses. Most cops find it boring, the complete antithesis to hot calls, but I always liked creeping around town on foot when there wasn't another living soul to be seen. I liked to imagine that just around the corner I'd come upon a burglary in progress. It really got my pulse racing even though I knew that I probably stood a better chance of being struck by lightning. But this "crisis rehearsal," always moving, always rehearsing, mentally entering various life-or-death situations and visualizing myself as the winner, was the way this one young cop kept sharp and occupied. Being a small-town cop in real life meant writing speeding tickets, taking nonviolent crime reports, and maybe making an occasional drug arrest, but when I was "walking the doors" it became, in my fantasy life, nothing less than exhilarating.

That night the air was crisp, and as the light snow fell it disappeared when it came in contact with the dark blue wool of my overcoat. The flakes that brushed against my face felt good, like the touch of cool, fluttering fingers. I kept stopping to look back at my footprints, struck by the fact that they were the only disfigurement in the pristine white carpet that covered the sidewalks and streets. When I stopped walking, I could actually hear the scudding whisper of the blanketing snow. I raised my head and watched as the glittering flakes drifted out of the dark sky; it felt as if I had wandered into some child's snow dome. I found myself smiling at all the images that accompanied the snowfall on this peaceful night.

It was then that I heard the shattering glass, muffled but unmistakable. My senses were on full alert, and I slipped into a recessed doorway, took off my glove, and unholstered my long-barreled .38. I took out my portable radio and was about to call in when I realized that I didn't know what to report. Glass breaking? Where? If I called in without the basic facts I'd sound like an idiot. I quickly slipped my radio back in its holder on my gun belt and set out to find the source of the noise.

My heart began to pound as I crept along the storefronts, my gun pointed at the ground, my breath coming out in foggy bursts. It wasn't until I got to the corner that I found it: a broken pane of glass above the lock on the door of an art supplies store. The adrenaline really kicked in when I saw the footprints in the new snow leading from the alley right to the door where I was standing. I knew that I had come upon a burglary in progress. I stood there, shaking from the cold, trying to visualize the layout of the store from my innumerable walk-throughs. There was also a rear door off the alley, and I figured if I took a position at the corner of the building, I could see anyone leaving from either door. I stealthily moved into position and yanked my radio out of its holder and breathlessly transmitted.

"Dispatch, this is Unit 2. I have a burglary in progress at Nassau Art. I need assistance."

The dispatcher was an old hairbag cop named Fields who had been made permanent desk man because of his love affair with Johnny Walker. He didn't answer. *Oh, shit,* I thought, *he must be bullshitting with the other guys and not paying attention to the radio.* I had just brought the radio up to my mouth to try again when I heard a sound in the alley behind the art store. It sounded like something metal scraping across slushy concrete. I quickly put my radio back on my belt and turned it off so that it wouldn't squawk and then stealthily moved in a crouch toward the mouth of the alley. I kept my revolver extended in front of me and took my eight-cell flashlight out of my belt. I didn't turn it on; I just held it in my left hand as I crept up alongside the building. All I could hear was my own labored breathing, which seemed to shatter the dead silence in this snow-covered limbo.

When I got to the mouth of the alley, I paused before I peered into the inky blackness. I heard nothing, so I decided, foolhardily or bravely I still don't know, to enter the narrow passage and cut off the escape route of my prey. No footprints were visible in the snow, so I knew that my quarry hadn't left. I was determined to catch the burglar, to show my squad that I had what it took to be a cop. I visualized myself parading my prisoner into the station and shoving him into a holding cell like a victorious hunter returning from the fields amid the admiring looks of his peers.

It was at that moment, when I was lost in a fantasy of heroism, that a specter bolted from the darkness like some demon from a horror movie. Then it was on me, screaming unintelligibly, and as my flashlight clattered out of my hand, I fired twice. The body smashed into me, knocking me to the ground. It squirmed on top of me, emitting a high-pitched keening noise that seemed hardly human. I felt the frigid snow invade my collar and chill my neck. I heard my own startled scream as I pushed the creature off me. I lurched to my feet and, stumbling and sliding in the wet snow, ran to the edge of the building and took cover. I was shaking violently as I pointed my pistol toward the crumpled figure that lay spasming in the darkening snow.

I yanked my radio out of my belt and yelled into it, "Officer needs help!" before I realized that I had turned it off. I holstered my pistol momentarily as my trembling fingers turned on the radio. "Officer needs help! Shots fired!"

"Where are you?" the dispatcher asked.

"The alley behind Nassau Art! I need backup and an ambulance! Shots fired!"

I heard another voice, that of my sergeant, cool and assured. "We're on the way."

I replaced the radio, and the silence seemed deafening. Then I could hear the moaning of the injured man in the alley. *I just shot him,* I thought, suddenly connecting his pain with my actions. It was a sound that I will never forget, half gurgling, half whimpering. I didn't move; I stood anchored to the spot until flashing red lights illuminated the snow-covered alley, turning it into a pulsating battlefield. The sergeant and the other patrolman on duty jumped out of the patrol car, guns drawn. They took up positions opposite me at the entrance to the alley and looked over to me for answers.

"I shot him" was all I could say.

We all heard the guttural moan at the same time. As the sergeant ran back to his car, the patrolman whispered to me, "Does he have a gun?"

I didn't answer; I just watched as the sergeant used the power-ful spotlight on his radio car to illuminate the passageway. We all saw the same thing, the twisted figure writhing in the snow, em-braced by a scarlet shadow.

"Did he shoot at you?"

It took me a moment to realize that the sergeant was standing next to me.

"What?"

"Does he have a fucking gun?! Did he shoot at you?!"

I looked down at my wool overcoat, almost expecting to see a bullet wound, but there was nothing, just the damp spots where the snow had soaked into the fabric.

"No . . . I don't think so."

"Why did you fire?"

"He . . . he came at me. He jumped me."

The sergeant looked at me for a long moment, his scrutinizing gaze nearly penetrating my flesh.

"Okay."

I felt disembodied as I watched him and the other patrolman approach the figure in the snow, guns drawn. The patrolman searched the man on the ground for weapons while the sergeant kept him covered. When the patrolman shook his head no, they both holstered their weapons and squatted down next to the figure.

"Sarge," I heard the patrolman say in a bewildered voice, "it's just Willy."

"Y-y-y-y-you," he said again. He was so worked up that his spit was turning into foam and collecting on his stubbled chin. He lurched for me, but I didn't flinch. I just sat there as the sweat oozed from my pores and ran in rivulets down my spine. He was right in front of me when he dropped his broom and his dirt collector clattered to the sidewalk. His mouth worked and his lips smacked together dryly as his red-rimmed eyes jammed into mine. Then, like a deflating balloon, he seemed to implode from the effort his hatred took, and he collapsed next to me on the bench. The passersby took no notice of us; to all the world we looked like two old friends sitting together in companionable silence: the onetime town cop, the onetime town delinquent casually reminiscing about the old days. Inside, my guts were clenching and I was back in the alley on that snowy night looking down at the gun in my hand as if it had fired of its own volition. I felt my hands begin to tremble, and I flattened my palms on my pant legs.

"W-w-w-w-w-w-why?"

I had been cleared of any wrongdoing in the shooting and had moved out of state and joined a different department within a few years of the incident. I had never answered that question, even to myself. Now, looking into those hollow eyes, I found myself taking off my sunglasses, looking him right in the face, and uttering the words I would have denied to anyone else.

"I was scared."

He looked at me for a long moment, his head at its awkward angle, his one good eye seeming to blister the side of my face. Then he seemed to spasm, and his head bobbed up and down. I realized he was nodding. His breath came out in a prolonged sigh.

"M-m-m-m-m-me, too."

So we sat in the floral-scented grasp of an intense summer's day, trapped in the memories of a winter's night when the snowflakes looked like tiny shooting stars but crimson-stained snow had tainted both our lives.

Honeysuckle, I thought as I tried to take a deep breath. *It brings back a lot of memories.*

THE MESSENGER

A Cop's Christmas Tale

DECEMBER 22: EVENING

PERCHED ON THE EDGE OF HIS FADED GREEN NAUGAHYDE couch, Pete sat in the dark and stared out of the picture window facing the street. He brought the amber-colored liquid to his lips and took a slow sip without even realizing he had done so. He was studying the house across the street as one would study a painting displayed in an art museum, reflecting on its form, its color, the twinkling lights that dangled from the roof like icicles, all the things that seemed to make it a real home, unlike his own. He knew the name of the people who lived there, the Andersons, but he didn't know them to talk to. Not anymore. There were the husband and wife, two school-age children, and a new infant who was always bundled up and gurgling in one of his parents' arms. They were mirror images, these two houses, of identical design and floor plan, but his lacked the foundation, beyond mortar and brick, that made a house a home. The house across the street was gaily and colorfully decorated in honor of the season, and the twinkling red lights that framed the picture window seemed to mock the austerity of his own dark and unadorned dwelling.

The bottle of scotch, which had been full an hour ago, now held only about three-quarters of its original content. As he took another sip the liquid burned his throat, but it brought a comforting and familiar warmth to his belly. He turned and glanced briefly at the mantel above his living room fireplace, where his sole acknowledgment of the Christmas season stood as a silent sentinel to his misery: a red felt Santa hat covering the top of a bottle of unopened scotch. He looked around the room, as if seeing it for the first time, absorbed his own halfhearted attempts at decoration, and wondered why he had even bothered. Christmas was for families, and his was gone. He gestured with his glass at the house across the street. "Merry Christmas," he whispered as he brought the glass to his lips. He downed the entire contents in one last gulp and staggered to bed.

DECEMBER 23: MORNING

Pete welcomed the oblivion of sleep, but when he awoke the next morning, his head throbbed and his body ached as he stumbled to the shower. It was the day before Christmas Eve, and though he didn't dislike the season, he wished it would pass him by unnoticed. It brought back too many memories, memories of a time when he looked forward to the holidays, looked forward to the family traditions and the love that filled his home. Now that seemed like a lifetime ago, maybe two lifetimes ago—those of his wife and daughter.

He pushed these troubling thoughts aside as the steaming water beat down on his face and chest, washing away the night's dim memories. Later, as he was wiping the steam from the bathroom mirror, he suddenly saw himself clearly and realized he wasn't someone he recognized anymore. He looked much older than his thirty-eight years. His brown hair was streaked with gray, and his forehead was home to deep racing furrows. The crow's feet at his eyes were much more pronounced than he remembered, and the lines around his mouth seemed to accentuate the perpetual frown he now wore. He quickly lathered his face with shaving cream, perhaps to hide the truth of what stared back at him. For a moment he closed his eyes, forced his thoughts to blur along with the image of himself, and steeled himself for the day ahead.

DECEMBER 23: AFTERNOON

His shift began at three o'clock, but he usually arrived early and was in the squadroom as the other officers began filtering in. He listened to them as they greeted one another, wisecracked, and talked about their plans for the holidays or compared notes on the calls they had answered the day before. The camaraderie Pete felt in the squadroom usually diluted his sense of loneliness. He was older than most of the patrolmen, and yet he felt a certain affinity for the young men and women, as if by mentoring them he could go back to a place and time when everything was new and challenging, a time when he possessed more enthusiasm than despair. Watching them, listening to them, Pete realized he still felt good about being a cop. Maybe it was the only thing he still felt good about, but it was something.

DECEMBER 23: EARLY EVENING

Pete worked the inner-city beat, a bleak and sullen expanse of urban decay that stretched for miles. As he cruised the streets, he realized once again that his was one of the few white faces to be seen in the area, yet he felt more at home there than he did in his own neighborhood. There was a deep chill in the air, and the swollen gray clouds overhead were threatening to disgorge their moisture in the form of either rain or snow. Pete kept his ear attuned to the radio, listening for his familiar call numbers, waiting to be dispatched to yet another scene of violence. Tragic calls were more common in the emotionally charged holiday season than during any other time of the year. He looked out his patrol car window, observing the familiar street-corner tableaus, still wondering at the clusters of young men who regarded him with open hostility. He'd spent years on the street, but he'd never gotten used to being hated, not for who he was but because of what he wore— a star on his chest. Yet, in an odd way, he was comforted by the constancy; it was just something he had come to expect.

The day became grayer, as did the streets. Darkness was creeping up, making the shadows longer and more forbidding, as Pete cruised through the back alleys, looking for any signs of disturbance. The back doors to the small businesses—a radiator repair shop, a taxidermist's studio, and a Chinese restaurant that had been closed for years—were bolted shut. Chain-link fencing surrounded hard-packed dirt lots filled with refuse and abandoned cars. Back there it could have been the end of the world; there was no sign of life. Then Pete thought he heard something. He stopped the car and turned off the engine so that he could listen more intently. It had almost sounded like a baby crying. As he got out of the car, he heard it again, a keening whimper. It seemed to be coming from the area near the trash container in the back of a dry-cleaning business.

He started toward the sound, his hand automatically grazing the butt of his pistol. He never knew what he was going to find, and this odd day, with the air still damp and heavy from the morning's rain, seemed portentous. He stepped behind the trash container and found a pile of empty crates. The sound had stopped, but he could feel a presence. This heightened his awareness of everything around him and set his senses tingling. In a quick and decisive motion he kicked one of the crates aside and found himself staring into the liquid brown eyes of a tiny gray puppy. It couldn't have been more than three months old. Its feet were too big for its shivering body, its short coat was oil-stained, and its ribs protruded, seeming to bend so sharply that they were about to snap.

Pete bent down, pulled his flashlight from his belt, and gently poked the creature, looking for signs of injury. A tuft of white fur jutted out from its chin, resembling the whiskers of an old man. It began to shake violently, peeing all over itself in fear, and Pete recoiled involuntarily at the sight of such abject misery. He'd seen it too often. The inner-city streets were full of these piteous creatures, and their lives were always short and painful, but there was nothing he could do; it was just another abandoned animal left to die on the street.

Pete sighed and started to return to his patrol car, but he heard the keening whimper again and stopped. He felt an odd stirring in his chest; it was as if that plaintive cry had been addressed directly to him. He turned back and peered again between the crates, right into the eyes of the orphaned puppy. When it saw him, the little creature stopped crying and seemed to gaze at him with the kind of undiluted hope he'd only seen before on the faces of children and madmen. He began moving the crates aside, expecting the trapped puppy to jump up and run away. But it didn't move; it just kept staring up at him. He felt the cold raindrops hit the back of his neck and slide down under the collar of his jacket, and he shivered involuntarily. The puppy mimicked him by shuddering, never breaking its expectant gaze. That did it: Pete bent over and scooped the puppy into his arms and carried it back to the patrol car.

Pete sat the puppy down on the passenger seat and turned the heater on high. Then he scrolled through his mobile computer, checking up on the calls in his sector, watching the puppy out of the corner of his eye.

"I'm not supposed to do this, you know. Let stray animals into my patrol car. You get dry, then you're on your way. Understood?"

Pete nodded as if agreeing with this decision, and then, surprisingly, the puppy's head bobbed up and down in its own version of a nod. Pete grinned, and the puppy bared its teeth, mimicking a smile. This time Pete laughed out loud.

"You're a funny dog, I'll give you that. And funny looking, too." He eyed the wild gray hair sprouting in tufts from the puppy's haunches, and the uneven ears—one drooped like a hound's, the other was pointed like a retriever's. He reached over and stroked the top of its head, and the puppy licked his fingers. He felt a lump in his throat before he pulled his hand away.

"Okay, that's enough." Pete got out of the car and walked around to the passenger's door and opened it wide.

"You're free to go. Beat it."

The puppy looked at him, yawned, and curled up in a ball on the passenger seat and closed its eyes.

"If I take you to the animal shelter, they're going to put you to sleep. They're overcrowded this time of year. At least you have a chance this way."

The puppy didn't move. Pete sighed and looked up at the cascading sky, feeling the rain on his face, and decided he simply couldn't leave this odd creature to its fate in the desolate alley. He shut the door and got back in the car.

"Where am I going to find a home for a dog like you? You're not cute. You might even be sick."

The puppy sleepily curled up next to him, resting its chin on his thigh, and Pete realized that he hadn't felt the simple warmth of another living being for a very long time.

It was a quiet night. It was as if all arguments had ceased in the spirit of the impending holiday. There were no domestic violence calls, no drive-by shootings, no bar fights, no convenience store robberies. It seemed, too, as if the streets were deserted and everyone was inside. For the first time in a long time, Pete was glad that nothing was going on. Usually he craved the excitement, the adrenaline rush—it kept his thoughts out of the past and firmly, by necessity, in the present—but tonight, with the puppy curled beside him, the heater on full blast, the comforting chatter of the dispatcher's voice, and the sound of Christmas music turned low on the radio, Pete was content. He surveyed the streets with a proprietary air, alert to everything around him, but most aware of his new companion.

Later in the evening, they were parked in the lot of a fast food restaurant. Pete was going through the entries in his address book while the puppy eagerly consumed five hamburger patties and lapped at the water in a makeshift bowl.

"I can't think of anybody who might give you a home." Actually, he'd come up with a few possible candidates, but for some reason he found himself dismissing them each in turn and not even calling to ask if they might be interested. The puppy, though, seemed not to care, and at the sound of Pete's voice it would turn and curl its lip in its odd little animal grin. That got a smile every time.

"I've still got half a shift to go. You don't really qualify as K-9, so what do you say if I drop you off at my house?"

Pete was thinking aloud, but the puppy wagged its tail so

violently in response that he found himself laughing for the second time that night. Here he was on patrol, all alone with an animal, talking to himself and laughing out loud. He wondered if he was losing it, but he didn't really care as he swung his patrol car around and headed toward his house. It was located out of his patrol route, but not by much, and he decided it would just take a minute and no one would be the wiser. On the way, he stopped at a convenience store and bought a bag of puppy food at twice the price of the supermarket version. He found himself wishing the clerk a Merry Christmas and whistling "O Come, All Ye Faithful" as he strode back to his patrol car. The puppy, its head reaching just to the bottom of the driver's side window, watched him as he approached, its stubby tail wagging furiously.

Pete pulled up in his driveway, scooped the puppy into his arms along with the bag of dog food, and practically bounded up the steps. This elevated mood was weird, he decided—maybe he was coming down with a fever or something. He looked down at the grinning puppy as he unlocked his door and thought, *No, it just feels nice to do a good deed, any good deed, at this time of the year.* Maybe the Christmas spirit had overtaken him after all.

He blocked off the doorway from the kitchen to the living room, left the puppy a huge bowl of food and water, spread newspaper all over the floor of the kitchen, and folded an old comforter into a bed.

"There you are," he said as he bent down and stroked the tiny creature's bristly head. Its hind end wiggled with pleasure. The half-empty bottle of scotch caught his eye; it was still on the coffee table where he had left it last night, but for once it didn't tempt him with its promise of oblivion. He realized he was looking forward to coming back home.

"I've got to get back to work," Pete said, almost as if the dog understood him. The puppy jumped up on its hind legs and licked his chin. Pete, without thinking, bent down and kissed it on the top of its head, much as he used to do to his small daughter before he went to work.

"I'll be back soon."

As he climbed into his patrol car he glanced over at the Andersons' house, sparkling with Christmas lights, and thought appreciatively that they'd done a great job.

DECEMBER 23: LATE EVENING

The rest of the shift passed quickly, more quickly than it had in months. In the squadroom at the end of shift briefing, Pete found himself again listening in on the other officers' plans for the holidays, but this time without that feeling of dread that had come over him before. He wished everyone a great Christmas with such bonhomie that he found some other officers looking at him speculatively. He knew why, too. He'd seen it before out on the street so many times. That forced, almost manic, gaiety of the holiday suicides-waiting-to-happen, as if their nearness to finality had made them giddy. Sergeant Taylor, an old friend, made his way across the squadroom toward him and said, "You got plans for Christmas, Pete? If you don't, you're welcome to come over to our house. Madeline's cooking up a turkey, and we've got her folks coming over from Phoenix. We'd love to have you join us."

Pete smiled and squeezed his friend's shoulder with affection. "Thanks, I appreciate the offer, but I've got a friend in town for the holidays."

Sergeant Taylor looked at Pete's face for a long time, his cop instincts stripping away any pretense, any falsehood. What he saw reassured him.

"Then you and your friend have a great Christmas, Pete."

Pete knew as he parked his car in the garage that he wouldn't be looking for a home for the puppy. The puppy belonged to him. He wondered if fate had led him into that alley, because that odd little creature was just what he needed. When he opened the door, he was certain he was right. The puppy was lying with its nose pressed to the base of the back door, having forsaken its warm bed, its food and water, to await Pete's return. He scooped the puppy up and held it, wiggling with glee, in his arms.

"You, puppy, still smell like garbage. What do you say about a bath?"

Half an hour later, Pete had the puppy in the sink, up to its chest in warm water, lathering it with baby shampoo. Since the puppy seemed to like the sound of his voice, he was singing a medley of all the Christmas carols he knew. Every time he raised his voice for emphasis, the puppy yowled in accompaniment. Pete was having fun. As he dried the tiny shivering body in a bath towel he decided it was a male, or at least he was pretty sure it was, and decided to name it Kringle. The name popped into his head with the same certainty as when he had first held his infant daughter.

"Her name is Amy," Pete told his wife in wonder and surprise.

She had looked at him solemnly and then at the sleeping child. "Yes, Pete, you're right. Her name is Amy."

He looked down at Kringle on his lap as he dried its whiskers and beard.

"Kringle. Do you like that? That's what I'm going to call you, Kringle." The puppy cocked its head and grinned.

DECEMBER 24, CHRISTMAS EVE: BEFORE DAWN

The dream came again. He had consumed no alcohol to drown the visions, nothing to medicate or subdue his raging imagination, so it came upon him full force like the SUV that had sailed through the intersection at seventy mph and broadsided his wife's compact car. He hadn't been in the car with his wife and daughter, but in his dreams he was there in the passenger seat. He saw the SUV coming, and he knew the driver was going to blow the red light. He tried to scream to Stacy to stop the car, but his screams were mute. She accelerated, headed into the intersection, into the beckoning green light. He only had time to turn and look at his young daughter behind him in the backseat, happily sounding out the words in her new Christmas book, before the SUV—and he could see it clearly now, a 1995 Chevy Suburban, midnight blue—slammed into their car with such force that they were airborne. He heard metal screeching against metal and glass exploding. The interior was wet with blood, Stacy's blood. He heard Amy choking in that moment before the compact hit the ground and the tires exploded and it plowed into the streetlight, imploding, crumpling in on itself with a horrible bellowing like a dying elephant. He smelled gasoline and the scotch, the familiar smell of scotch, very expensive scotch, from the bottle that slipped from the drunken SUV driver's lap and shattered on the floorboards. Then he felt the tremendous pressure on his chest where the steering wheel had crushed his sternum and snapped his ribs as it had Stacy's, and he tried to turn in his seat to look at his daughter, but his neck, like Stacy's, was broken and his mouth and eyes were filled with blood.

It was always at this point in his terrible dream that Pete knew he was dreaming and tried to wake up, but it was like he was trapped underwater and could only faintly see the rays of sun—the light from the digital clock—penetrating the darkness. Then his dream changed to his own memory of that night. He had been working when he got the call and had driven like a maniac to the hospital, but they were both DOA. He had gone to the scene, to the intersection, to see if he could be closer to them there, there where their spirits had left their bodies and drifted into the night sky toward heaven, or so he hoped and believed. But he felt nothing but a terrible sense of loss as he watched the traffic officers measure the skid marks and take photographs. They didn't pay much attention to him. He was in uniform; they thought he was just looking over yet another fatal traffic accident scene. They had no idea that it was his family who had died there. He had stood looking at the pulverized compact—it didn't even resemble a car any longer—and it was then that he noticed the bits and pieces of Christmas wrapping paper all over what had been the backseat. They had been Christmas shopping, his wife and daughter, and were on their way home. He looked down at the oil-stained pavement and saw a Santa tag near the toe of his boot. It said, "To Daddy, From Amy." That was always when he awoke screaming.

This time, though, the puppy was sitting on his chest, frantically licking his face, licking the tears from his cheeks, licking the sweat from his brow. He struggled to sit up in bed; he tried to push the animal away.

"Kringle! Stop! Stop it!" The puppy was relentless. He pushed it too hard and it fell to the floor with a yelp, and in a moment he was beside it on the floor, scooping it into his arms, cuddling it, comforting it against his bare chest. The puppy was trembling; he was shivering in his boxer shorts.

"I'm sorry," he whispered to the strange little animal as he stroked its head, though when he spoke he was looking at the photograph of his wife and daughter that he kept by the bed. He crawled back under the covers, letting Kringle come with him and curl like a ball against the back of his knees, and he fell into a deep and surprisingly untroubled sleep for the first time in five years.

DECEMBER 24, CHRISTMAS EVE: LATE MORNING

When Pete awoke, Kringle was sleeping on the pillow right next to his head. He opened his eyes, the puppy opened his, and Pete was greeted with a flick of a tongue across the bridge of his nose. The puppy's liquid eyes were luminous and full of trust. Pete found himself returning the little creature's teeth-baring grin and scratching it behind its fur-tufted ears.

After dressing, Pete took Kringle out into the backyard so the puppy could do its business. He watched the little creature running around, lurching and gamboling as it explored the entire backyard, sniffing so intently that more than once it had an attack of sneezing. Standing there, Pete realized that the house could do with a coat of paint and that he hadn't mowed the lawn in quite a while. The swing set that he had put together so happily the last year of Amy's life was rusting—no child had used it since. Maybe if he cleaned it up the Andersons might want it. For the first time in years he looked at things straight on and not obliquely; he wondered how long it had been since he had even noticed his own backyard.

"Kringle!" he called. "Come on, boy!" He whistled, and the puppy bounded to him, tongue lolling, eyes bright. Pete laughed and reached down and picked up the squirming creature, being careful to hold the muddy paws away from his robe.

"We've got some things to do before I go to work."

Pete and his new companion had breakfast together in the

kitchen. Pete cooked himself ham and eggs, and Kringle ate his puppy chow with a liberal portion of ham and eggs as well, and then man and dog went together out to the front of the house.

For two hours Pete strung around the house the Christmas lights he'd stored in the garage. He took special care to festively encircle the bay window with red, white, and green lights. He had pulled them from a top shelf in the garage, a box illustrated with a caricature of Santa labeled GRISWOLD FAMILY CHRISTMAS SUPPLIES in Stacy's familiar printing. He'd felt something catch in his throat, but he hadn't let himself put back the box and retreat into the house, into the bottom of a glass, as he had done in the previous years. Now, as he worked, Kringle sat near the bottom of the ladder, never running toward the street, just content to be near Pete, his food-swollen belly making him look more like a normal puppy and less like a bag of bones.

When Mr. Anderson came out of his front door and saw Pete up on his ladder, he stopped short and looked over for a long moment, until Pete noticed him and waved. About an hour later, Mr. Anderson, trailed by his six-year-old, Cindy, and his nine-year-old, Max, came strolling across the street. He stood there for an hour, giving advice, assisting like neighbors do, while the two kids played tag with Kringle on the lawn.

"We haven't talked much, Pete, have we? Not since . . ." Mr. Anderson cleared his throat awkwardly, then looked over at the happy kids frolicking with the puppy.

Pete knew what he was about to say. Mr. Anderson's daughter was now the same age that Amy had been when she died; his son, Max, had been a toddler then. The two couples, the Griswolds and the Andersons, and their small children had been friendly, but after Stacy and Amy died, Pete had walked stiffly up his walkway after the funeral and shut the door behind him. Five years had passed as if they had simply evaporated. Pete looked down at his neighbor and saw that he was older, too; streaks of gray shot through his hair at the temples, and there were deepening furrows in his cheeks. It was odd, but Pete suddenly felt sympathy for his neighbor, the man he never got to know as an individual, never shared a beer with on some rainy afternoon in the garage while the family was snug in the house. *There are different kinds of losses,* thought Pete, *and some are missed opportunities.*

"Yeah," Pete said, and smiled. "I've been working way too much. But I was looking at your house and thinking this year I was going to just have to make the time and get with the festivities."

Mr. Anderson searched Pete's face for signs of irony or sadness or something hidden and festering, but Pete knew how to keep emotions from breaking the surface; it was part of his job, after all. Mr. Anderson nodded and returned the smile as Pete climbed down off the ladder. He appraised Pete's efforts and said approvingly, "It's getting there."

Pete laughed. "It'll have to do for this year. I've got to get ready for work."

"Maybe next year I can help you get an early start."

Pete reached out and shook his hand. "Come by for a beer sometime, Sam."

Mr. Anderson nodded. "I will, Pete. I'm off all next week. I'll mosey on by."

He turned and strolled back across the lawn, calling to his children, and the two kids reluctantly released their new playmate back into Pete's custody. Pete scooped the puppy up and held it against his chest and stroked its ears as he watched the trio disappear into their house. Pete didn't feel the sharp pain below his rib cage that he usually did, that stab of envy and loss; he just felt happy for the Andersons. He looked down into Kringle's adoring eyes and wondered if it really was this easy or if this swelling of "goodwill to all" would burst and leave him worse off than he was before.

"Whatever happens, Kringle, I'm glad I brought you home."

As Pete walked through the house getting ready for work, Kringle was right behind him, his stubby tail wagging furiously, his paws skidding and sliding on the wooden floorboards, his tongue lolling happily. Pete looked into the mirror to shave and was startled. Was it his imagination or did he look younger? The crow's feet seemed to have faded, and his haggardness was gone. The nightmares had come, but he hadn't anesthetized himself with alcohol and afterward had slept deeply.

As he was about to leave, he blocked off the kitchen, spread newspapers on the floor, and hugged the wiggling little dog.

"I'll see you later tonight, little guy. You be the guard dog, okay?"

As he slipped out the back door, he would have sworn he saw disappointment in the puppy's luminous eyes, but he chided himself for being fanciful. Halfway to his car he heard a single thin wail of despair from the little creature, and he had to force himself to get in and drive away. All he could think of was coming back home.

DECEMBER 24, CHRISTMAS EVE: AFTERNOON

Pete sat in his usual place in the briefing room at the station. He didn't notice that some of the other officers had observed the change in his demeanor. They couldn't quite put their finger on it, but something was different about Officer Pete Griswold. Maybe he seemed more animated than usual; maybe he wasn't quite so withdrawn. A few commented to each other. One patrol officer joked that he hoped Griswold wasn't evidencing that false high elation that accompanies holiday suicides. Sergeant Taylor overheard this and looked closely at Pete as he was walking out.

"How you doing, Pete?"

"I'm good, Sarge. I'm good."

Sergeant Taylor was damned if he could see otherwise.

"You're seeing your friend tonight, Pete, aren't you?"

"I sure am, Sarge. Thanks for asking. Merry Christmas."

"Merry Christmas, Pete."

The sergeant shrugged and hit the street himself.

DECEMBER 24, CHRISTMAS EVE: LATE AFTERNOON

The shift progressed without any major incidents, though the routine calls and traffic accidents kept Pete busy enough. While he was standing on the side of a rain-slick highway jotting down the salient details of a noninjury fender bender, he wondered how little Kringle was doing. He glanced up at the leaden sky and felt glad that the little animal was safe in his kitchen and not still huddled behind some crates in a downtown alley. As he put the reflectorized cone back in the trunk of his patrol car, he decided it would be all right to go home and check on the animal. Then his radio crackled to life and dispatched him to a disturbance call involving a juvenile on the Westside. He slammed the trunk, nodded to the tow truck driver, and acknowledged the call over the radio.

The Westside was mostly residential and made up of small but proud homes populated by a generation that had witnessed the civil rights movement, the promise of John F. Kennedy, and the dignity of Martin Luther King. He found himself wondering about the occupants of each small house he passed—if the optimism of that idealized time still prevailed or if something essential had been lost. He had grown up in a house like these; maybe he was still recognizable as one of the small boys in dungarees who played baseball with the other kids on the street in the empty lot. Pete shuddered, shaking off the past. Twilight was approaching, and with it the temperature dropped. The skies continued to drain themselves onto the slick streets below.

Pete found the address easily and parked two doors down from the faded white clapboard house. As he walked up the sidewalk, he noticed a 1970s Cadillac parked in the carport. It was obvious from the cobwebs cascading down from the wheel wells to the cement below that the car hadn't been driven in years. The house, Pete noted as he approached the front door, had once been a source of pride for the owners, but now it wasn't being kept up. The paint was peeling, the sidewalk was cracked, and the lawn was patchy with hard-packed dirt that looked like fading brown scabs on the struggling grass. Pete thought wryly that this house looked like his own life.

He was still distracted by his thoughts when the door swung open. His hand went to the butt of his gun; his fingers unsnapped his holster by instinct, his body tense, heart racing. No cop liked being surprised. He relaxed when he saw the woman inside.

She was tiny, maybe four-ten, and at first he thought she was a child, maybe the juvenile in question. Then she peered around the door so that her face was harshly illuminated by the streetlight at the curb. She was at least seventy years old, with wizened features and thick glasses in heavy black frames that made her eyes look far too large for her tiny head. Her cocoa-colored face was haloed by wispy white hair pulled back in a loose bun at the nape of her neck, and the clothes that hung on her thin frame seemed to belong to another, more robust woman.

"Thank you for coming, Officer. I didn't know what else to do." She stood back, and Pete stepped inside into the warmth of the house.

This wasn't the way he usually did things; he usually asked questions while getting his bearings, letting his gut tell him how to proceed. This time something propelled him unquestioningly inside. The first thing he noticed was the smell of fresh pine from the little Christmas tree, which mingled with the delicious smell of roasting turkey. The house was spotless, and the furniture, surely store-bought at Sears when Kennedy was president, was threadbare but sturdy. There didn't seem to be anyone else in the small house.

She motioned him to the floral-print sofa and perched on the edge of an easy chair, facing him. He didn't sit; he stood and waited as she studied his face and he studied hers. Finally, apparently satisfied with what she saw, she touched her chest with her fist and said, "Ella Cooper."

"Officer Griswold, ma'am. Pete Griswold."

She glanced down the hallway that led to the rear of the house.

"Tabitha has locked herself in the bathroom and won't come out."

Pete nodded. "And Tabitha is?"

"My granddaughter. She's nearly seven."

"Do you have any reason to believe she's in any danger right now?"

"No, Officer . . . that's not what . . . that's not why I called." She reached into her sweater pocket and pulled out a key and held it up so that he could see it. "I can get in the bathroom if I need to."

Pete looked down the hall and then closely at Mrs. Cooper, then sat on the floral-print sofa, adjusting his gear belt so that he could sit comfortably.

"Does she live here with you?"

Mrs. Cooper nodded. "Her mother left her with her daddy a week after she was born. Her daddy is my son. He drank himself to death." She kept nodding to herself as if she were trying to reconcile something so horrible with the benevolence of her surroundings.

Pete, through experience, knew her story wasn't all that uncommon. "When did he die, ma'am?"

"Almost this time last year. Near Christmas."

"What happened today?"

"We had just come back from church. We were there all morning. St. Joan's, just across from the Justice Center. Do you know it?"

Pete nodded.

"Tabitha sings in the children's choir. Oh, she sings like an angel, that child!" She smiled and handed him a framed photograph of a thin little girl with cornrows sticking up in all directions and a big toothy grin. Then tears flooded her eyes, and she set her glasses in her lap. She dabbed at her eyes with a tissue she pulled from her sweater sleeve. "I told Tabitha that her father was with Jesus. That He had called him home to the Lord. I heard her asking Jesus—the carved wooden Jesus above the altar—to let her daddy come back for Christmas. She was down on her knees, Officer, praying to Jesus to let her daddy come for a visit and promising that if he did, she wouldn't ask for anything else." Mrs. Cooper pinched her eyes closed and then opened them, looking right at Pete. "Maybe I was wrong to tell her that. My son was a weak man, but his little girl loved him so. While we were walking home I told her that Jesus loved her and heard her prayer but he couldn't let her daddy come back. Not even for a little while."

"That's when she locked herself in the bathroom?"

Mrs. Cooper nodded, twisting the tissue in her lap. Pete looked again at the picture of the little girl. He understood how it felt to have your most fervent prayers unanswered, to feel as though by locking a door you could lock out all the hurt and disappointment and loss that threatened to overwhelm you.

"What is it exactly, Mrs. Cooper, that you want me to do?"

She stood up and walked over to him. They were almost eye to eye even though he was seated. She touched the back of his hand with her smooth, dry fingers, and her magnified gaze seemed to pierce right through him.

"Just talk to her, Officer. Maybe you will know better than me what to say."

Pete had talked suicidal people off of rooftops and cornered robbers out of hiding. He had talked people out of their rage and need for revenge; he had talked adolescents out of their despair. Talking was what cops did—very little of life on the street involved pointing a gun at someone's chest or wrestling people to the floor to handcuff them. You talked. That's what you did. You reasoned and cajoled and offered sympathy and gave a face to authority. But for some reason Pete had to take a deep breath and gather himself to go and talk to a little girl who had a beef with Jesus.

He reached out and took the key from Mrs. Cooper and headed down the hallway to the closed bathroom door. He passed both small bedrooms on his way; Mrs. Cooper's was a combination bedroom and sewing room. Pete guessed that she took in mending and ironing to supplement her Social Security. He breathed deep, catching the heavy scent of lavender hand lotion and the pungent odor of mothballs. Tabitha's bedroom was spartan and neat. The twin bed was made, and there were some used Dr. Seuss books on a card table and a single doll seated on a rickety chair. A picture of Jesus hung in a frame on the wall next to a fuzzy picture of a lanky man with a pack of Camels in his shirt pocket. He held a tiny child who was grinning, her arms wrapped around his neck.

Pete knocked on the bathroom door.

"Tabitha?"

There was no noise at all until a tiny voice said, "Who are you?"

"I'm Officer Pete Griswold from the police department. Your grandmother is worried about you, and I'd like to make sure you're okay."

"I'm okay."

"Can you please open the door so that we can talk? I'd really like to talk to you. Please."

Nothing happened for a minute, and Pete looked down at the key in his hand. Then he heard a rattle at the door as the locking mechanism disengaged. He dropped the key in his pocket as the door swung open to reveal the child in Mrs. Cooper's picture. She looked exactly the same, only she wasn't grinning. Dried tears stained her cheeks, and her nose was running. Her complexion was café au lait, her delicate features almost Asian. He wondered what her mother had looked like. He wondered if she had tried to find her face in her father's much as his own daughter—the image of her mother—had tried to do when he read her a bedtime story. The little girl, Tabitha, looked up at him, solemn and unafraid.

"Who called you?" she asked him, her big eyes taking him in, much as her grandmother's had.

Pete was not prone to impulses or flights of fancy; he was always rational and levelheaded on the job, but the last two days had shaken him up. Without missing a beat he said, "Jesus called me. He asked me to come over and talk to you."

Her eyes grew impossibly large, and she opened the door wide and stared at him.

"You know Jesus?"

"I work for him."

She looked at his uniform, her eyes stopping at his belt.

"Why do you have a gun?"

"So Jesus never has to carry one. I help to keep all the little children safe."

He watched her thinking about this for a moment, and then she seemed to accept what he was saying. She reached out and took his hand, and the two walked into her bedroom and sat side by side on her bed looking up at the two pictures on the wall. He indicated the one next to Jesus' portrait.

"Is that your daddy?"

Tabitha nodded.

"Jesus tells me you've been praying for your daddy to come home for Christmas."

She nodded again. Pete reached into his back pocket and took out his wallet and reached behind his driver's license for the picture of his wife and daughter. He was always aware of its being there, yet he almost never looked at it, preferring the soft edges of memory to the razor clarity of a photograph. Now, as he held the small photograph in his hand so that Tabitha could look at it, too, he studied their familiar and beloved faces, and for once he was comforted by their smiles, captured and preserved in a moment in time. Tabitha leaned over his arm and looked closely at the picture and then up at Pete.

"This is my family, Tabitha. They live with Jesus, too. But it's okay."

Pete hadn't been to church in five years, and he had never paid close attention to what the minister was saying during the sermon, just enjoyed the serenity and the ceremony, but he told Tabitha all about heaven and how beautiful it was with its tall trees and wide lakes and fields of flowers. He told her about how all the animals lived together in peace, the lions with the lambs, and how all the people who lived there with Jesus and with the Heavenly Father, like her daddy and his own wife and daughter, were content and in no pain. Their afterlife would be perfect except that they worried about those they had left behind. We will all be together in the end, Pete told the little girl, but until then we are still here because we have things to accomplish, good deeds to do, joy to experience, and love to give. That's what they wanted for us. That's what her daddy wanted for her.

As Pete looked into the child's wide eyes, he thought he could lie with the best of them. He had once persuaded a young man to take the barrel of his .357 out of his mouth and drop the weapon on the floor by convincing him that he didn't kill his girlfriend, that she was okay, that he'd just talked to her and she was on her way to the hospital, even though she was lying just outside the room with half her head gone. And he'd looked a terrified and dying man who had been shot during a bank robbery right in the eye and told him he would be fine, that the ambulance was on the way and his wound wasn't all that bad, even as the blood pooled around him, encompassing the two of them like victims in a flood. The fear had left the man's eyes, and he had died peacefully in expectation of recovery. Yes, Pete could lie without compunction. He could work for Jesus and there could be a heaven if that's what it took to keep a lonely child from locking herself away in the bathroom to cry.

He felt Tabitha's small fingers wrapping around his own. He

looked up and saw Mrs. Cooper standing in the doorway. Then he saw how the tears from his eyes had spotted his uniform pants.

"Officer Griswold is telling you God's truth, Tabitha."

"I know, Grandma."

In one blinding moment, Pete realized that that's exactly what he was doing. For if the cardinal virtues were Faith, Hope, and Charity, what he was telling this serious little girl was as close to truth as one mortal man could ever come.

DECEMBER 24, CHRISTMAS EVE: LATE EVENING

All the rest of the shift, Pete found his thoughts straying between his new puppy at home and the little girl and her grandmother. He was feeling things, as if the anesthesia were finally wearing off. That dull ache of loss he had been trying to suppress for the past five years came back, along with happier emotions, as if he had once again joined the land of the living. He didn't know what to make of it; it was if a dam had burst so suddenly that all the people living beneath its vast walls weren't afforded the chance to get away. He was being bounced along downstream in a roaring river, and for the first time in years he let himself go along with it. Pete knew he was headed toward some bright light, the proverbial one at the end of the tunnel, but he didn't know if he would finally be set free and allowed to live, perhaps in emotional poverty but alive, or if he would end the holiday season with his gun in his mouth. For the last five years he had barely avoided the latter; this was the first time he allowed himself some flicker of hope. As he took the statement of a convenience store clerk who had been robbed of $160 at knifepoint but not hurt, he realized no one saw what was going on inside of him. He listened and nodded and presented an air of calm authority. He was a damn fine cop and he knew it. He had long thought that if he could only keep his uniform on day and night, he would be fine. But there had come the endless nights, the bottles of scotch and the nightmares.

The clerk reached out and shook Pete's hand and nodded at the teenaged suspect handcuffed in the back of Pete's patrol car.

"Thank you for getting here so quick, Officer. I feel like you saved my life. You have a nice Christmas, will you?"

Pete smiled. "I will. You, too." As he drove back to the station, he thought he just might.

DECEMBER 25, CHRISTMAS: VERY EARLY MORNING

When Pete finally finished his paperwork, it was nearly 2:00 A.M. He lingered for a long while, talking to the other cops who came in, listening to everyone's plans for the holidays, the anecdotes from the street that night. The camaraderie was high, and Pete felt good. Best of all, he wasn't dreading going home.

When he drove into his driveway at a little after 3:00 A.M., the entire block was quiet, but the outside Christmas lights were on in the majority of the houses, making his neighborhood look like one of those depicted on a holiday card. He opened his back door, and Kringle bounded into his arms, licking his face in a paroxysm of delight, yipping and wiggling so that Pete could barely hang on to the slippery little creature.

"Whoa, Kringle! Take it easy—you missed me, did you?"

He took the puppy into the backyard so it could relieve itself, then filled its bowl with fresh puppy chow. After he cleaned up the soiled newspapers and turned on the inside lights, Pete picked up the puppy again, holding it to his chest and stroking its head as he went into the living room. The unopened bottle of scotch with its red felt Santa hat was just as he had left it. He picked it up and looked at the label; it was an expensive brand, a gift from a cop on his squad, and Pete had been saving it for a special occasion. He took off the red felt hat and set the bottle back down.

"Here, boy, this looks like it might just fit." Pete pulled the hat down over the puppy's head and tied it loosely around its neck. Kringle looked up at him adoringly and started chewing happily on the white pom-pom. Pete had to laugh—the puppy looked like an orphan in a Dickens tale. He slipped the warm creature inside his coat, zipped it up so the puppy would stay warm, flipped on his outside lights, and stepped outside.

Pete stood in front of his house, ablaze with Christmas lights, and was captivated by how beautiful it looked. There was a sense of peace, of serenity, on the whole block. He looked at each house in turn, taking in the festivity and the solemnity of the lights, letting the beauty of the season sweep over him. As if on cue, the rain that had been threatening all evening came down, but as snowflakes, huge flakes that fell like tiny angels alighting.

"See that, Kringle? It's going to be a white Christmas."

The puppy, its red hat gaily askew, licked his chin in response and grinned. Pete looked over at the Andersons' house and realized it wasn't so different from his—not anymore. His eye was drawn to the manger scene, illuminated in such a way that it looked as if candlelight were being emitted from the miniature barn. The three wise men were making their way up the lawn, gifts in hand; Joseph and Mary were kneeling, looking in wonder at the tiny infant in the makeshift crib filled with straw.

"That's the baby Jesus, Kringle. He didn't have it easy in the beginning, either." Pete's thoughts turned to the call he had answered earlier in the day, to the, little girl, Tabitha, and her diminutive grandmother. They were doing the best they could with what little they possessed, even though many of their prayers went unanswered. He thought of the tiny tree in the old woman's living room, decorated with hand-sewn ornaments and colored string. There hadn't been many presents under the tree, but there was love in that house; he had felt it the moment he stepped through the door.

Pete realized he wasn't the least bit tired. In fact, he felt energized. He knew there was something he had to do.

Back in the house, Pete turned on a Christmas CD by Tony Bennett and let the crooner's familiar voice fill the rooms. He lit a fire in the fireplace and tidied up the house, washing all the dishes and even changing the sheets on his bed. Everywhere he went, Kringle was right on his heels. He was vacuuming, having finished his bedroom and the living room, and was running the machine up and down the hallway carpet—with Kringle barking at the "beast" the entire time—when he stopped outside the door to the second bedroom. This had been Amy's room, and he had left it as she had left it when she had gone off Christmas shopping with her mom five long years ago. He opened the door, flipped on the light, and looked inside. It was cold inside the room—he had shut the vents to the floor heater since the room was unused—and everything was covered with a thin layer of dust. He hadn't been in there in a long time. He hadn't left it as it was as a shrine to his daughter, or because he couldn't accept that she wouldn't be coming back; he had just shut the door and decided not to deal with it. She was gone, and all her vitality had gone with her; this was dead space, and nothing in there brought her back to him more vividly than his memories. Kringle stepped cautiously inside the room, growling in a high-pitched puppy way, sensing that something was wrong in the room—there was no recent scent of human occupation.

"It's okay, boy. It's okay."

He stepped inside and looked around. He and Stacy had joked that they were spoiling their only daughter, and he saw that it was true; her room was overflowing with all the belongings of a beloved child. There were toys of every imaginable sort—dolls and games and puzzles and art supplies. Books and costume jewelry and every kind of child's sporting equipment imaginable, from soccer to basketball to ice-skating. Pete spotted an ant farm, a collection of Barbies, and a pogo stick. Stuffed animals, including an entire family of teddy bears, covered the bed—every Sesame Street character was present and accounted for. A Tiny Tot Macintosh computer sat prominently on her desk. Amy had been looking at pictures of butterflies, Pete remembered. She had insisted on showing him a monarch butterfly on her screen before he read her a bedtime story. Clothes overflowed from the closet—dresses and outfits, all matching and coordinated, and almost-new sweaters bulging from the chest of drawers.

In his own bedroom, where he and Stacy had slept, her things were still there but pushed aside from his. Gradually his own things had taken over the medicine cabinet, the dresser, and the night tables by the bed. This was different—it was as if time had simply stopped at Amy's door. Pete felt a wave of grief sweep over him, and the loss punched at his heart with such ferocity that he had to lean back against the doorjamb to steady himself, but he didn't back away and shut the door. He looked down at Kringle, who was sitting at his feet, gazing up at him, wagging that stubby tail.

"It's time, Kringle. But you're going to have to help me."

DECEMBER 25, CHRISTMAS: DAWN

Pete closed and latched the tailgate on his pickup truck just as the sky started to lighten from the rays preceding the sun over the eastern horizon. The snow had fallen steadily all night, and now the quiet neighborhood was blanketed with a layer of powdery snow. Snow seldom stayed on the ground long in this part of the country, so he knew that he was seeing something that might be gone when the rest of the residents awoke from their slumber. He stood and breathed deep and watched as the sun took its first tentative steps into the new day. Kringle was asleep in a cardboard box on the back porch. The game little dog had followed Pete back and forth from the house to the truck for most of the night, but when it had started to yawn and stumble, Pete had taken the old comforter and made a bed for the puppy on the porch where it could see Pete's comings and goings. Now the little creature was burrowed deep into the warm embrace of the heavy blanket. Pete could just make out the tuft of wiry hair between its lopsided ears.

Pete went inside to shower and dress; he still wasn't tired or sleepy. He knew it would catch up to him, but for now he was being propelled forward with an adrenaline high that felt like hopeful anticipation. Again, as he shaved, he looked at himself closely in the mirror, but he didn't see the details of his face this time; he saw only the outline of his form, as if he were ready to be filled in again with substance and with color.

He stopped at the door to Amy's room as he headed toward the back door and looked inside. The room wasn't cold anymore, but it was empty. Everything inside, including the furniture, was gone. Pete thought that he would make the room into an office for himself, or maybe a guest room. He would take his time to decide.

Pete picked up Kringle and hugged the yawning little puppy. "It's my day off, Kringle. You can come with me, okay? We've got some errands to run, and then we'll come back and celebrate the holiday in style. Steak, maybe? Something we both like. Come on, boy."

Pete drove toward the Westside with Kringle sitting beside him on the pickup's bench seat, head resting on Pete's thigh. When he pulled up and parked in front of the white clapboard house it was light outside, but barely dawn. The house was dark, the 1970s Cadillac seeming like the ghost of Christmas past. Pete parked the truck and looked at the house, wondering aloud to the little animal if this was such a good idea. Kringle just yawned and sat up, licking his new master's hand where it rested on the wheel. Pete was almost ready to start the truck again and drive off when the front door opened and he saw Tabitha's face peering out. That did it. Pete climbed out of the truck and strode toward the house, his boots crunching on the new snow.

Tabitha was wearing a man's sweater over her pajamas. The hem fell all the way to her knees, and the arms were rolled up so that it looked as if she had pom-poms at her wrists.

"Do you remember me, Tabitha?"

She nodded and looked past him toward his truck. He followed her gaze. He knew she was looking for someone else.

"Are you working for Jesus?" she asked him. The hope in her voice hit Pete like a blow, but he forced his expression to remain impassive.

"No. Today I'm working for Santa Claus." He held up a piece of paper in his hand and pretended to read. "Your name is Tabitha Cooper, right? I don't want to deliver all this stuff to the wrong house."

She nodded at him wonderingly just as her grandmother appeared behind her, belting her robe. She smiled at him in recognition, but he saw she was confused.

"Officer Griswold?"

"Merry Christmas, ma'am. Request permission to deliver this Santa Claus consignment to Miss Tabitha Cooper."

He watched her as she looked out at the truck, then back at him, then at her granddaughter eagerly awaiting her reply. He knew she wanted to politely refuse what felt like charity, what must have seemed like pity, but then he felt her searching his own face, and he knew she saw his need. He felt his face flush and his eyes fill with tears.

"You may," the old woman said as she reached out and touched his hand. "But there is a condition."

Pete nodded.

"You will have Christmas supper with us."

"I'm sorry, I really can't."

"Please. We don't have a lot, but we have more than enough for three."

Pete smiled and then looked back at the pickup truck, where Kringle was standing on his hind legs looking worriedly in their direction.

"My problem is that I've got a friend with me."

Mrs. Cooper looked toward the truck. "My word, what kind of a creature is that?"

"It's a puppy!" Tabitha cried. "Please, grandma, let the puppy come in, too!"

Pete stared at the little girl. It was the first time he had seen her animated, as excited as only children can be, had even seen her smile.

"Of course," said Mrs. Cooper. "The puppy is welcome, too."

Before either of them could stop her, Tabitha ran down the snow-covered walk in her bare feet, opened the truck door, and scooped Kringle into her arms.

"Tabitha!" her grandmother called, but she was already back

up the walk, the puppy grinning happily in its odd way, bouncing in the child's arms as she darted inside the house.

DECEMBER 25, CHRISTMAS DAY: LATE MORNING

Pete had finally finished. He had unpacked all the boxes that he had loaded into the back of the pickup truck during the night, and he had reassembled everything that needed assembling. He was careful to keep the Dr. Seuss books prominent on the desk and to leave the two pictures on the wall clearly visible. He stood back and surveyed what he had done. Everything that had been in Amy's room was now in this little bedroom, and it seemed overflowing with riches.

Mrs. Cooper kept herself busy all morning in the kitchen, and the house was filled with the wonderful smell of baking cookies, roasting turkey, and a scent he couldn't identify—cinnamon, maybe, something that made his mouth water. Tabitha had sat on the living room floor playing with Kringle while watching Pete make trip after trip from the pickup truck to her room.

"What's in that box?" she would ask each time Pete passed her. Each time Pete would respond, "You know I can't spoil a Christmas surprise. You want me to get fired?" Each time the solemn little girl would smile at him and shake her head.

Now everything was ready.

"Okay, Tabitha, you can come and look."

Tabitha came tentatively down the hall, Kringle at her heels, Mrs. Cooper following, wiping her hands on her apron. Before she reached the door, Pete put his hands over her eyes and maneuvered her into the middle of the room.

"Are you ready?" He could feel her nodding beneath his fingers.

"Okay . . . Merry Christmas!" He pulled his hands away and she gasped.

Mrs. Cooper came in the door behind them and cried out, "My Lord! . . . Oh, my . . . Tabitha, thank Officer Griswold."

Tabitha burst into tears and ran from the room. Pete, taken aback, stared after her; Mrs. Cooper was as surprised as he was. Kringle went bounding after the little girl.

"What's wrong?" Pete asked Mrs. Cooper. She shook her head and clutched at her throat. He went after the child.

Pete found Tabitha in Mrs. Cooper's bedroom. She was sitting on the floor between the bed and the wall, scooted as far back into the corner as she could go. She was crying, and Kringle was jumping up on her chest, trying to lick her face.

"No, Kringle! Stop it!"

Pete sat on the edge of the bed and pulled Kringle away. He waited until she stopped crying. He handed her a tissue and waited, holding Kringle on his lap. She glanced up at him, then looked away.

"Thank you, Officer Griswold."

"Tabitha, what's wrong?"

She shrugged and looked down at the floor and then up into his eyes.

"It's . . . it's *too* much."

Pete, so worried that he had done something terribly wrong, burst into laughter.

"I understand. It *is* too much. But there's a trick to dealing with things like this. Do you know what it is?"

She shook her head.

"You don't want to look at everything directly and all at once. You have to ease yourself into it. Do you understand? Listen, what you need to do is this." He held his hands over his eyes and spread his fingers so that he could see her through the cracks. "You take things in like this—a little at a time. You see too much? Just lower the shades until it's comfortable." He pinched his fingers shut so that he couldn't see anything, then opened them a crack. "That's the trick. You want to control what you see until you are ready to look at it head-on." He dropped his hands. "See?"

"Where did you learn this?"

"Just in my own life. But it works."

She nodded and looked down at her own hands, stretched her fingers as if evaluating them. He reached down and took one of her hands in his.

"Your grandmother has supper on the table. Are you ready?" Tabitha got to her feet, and Pete, Tabitha, and Kringle walked together into the dining room.

DECEMBER 25, CHRISTMAS DAY: AFTERNOON

It was a wonderful Christmas dinner. There was roast turkey and stuffing and cranberries and hot rolls and a green bean casserole. There was ice-cold eggnog and homemade apple pie for dessert. Pete felt sleepy in the warm little house, but content, as if he were dreaming he was someone else. Mrs. Cooper said grace and thanked the Lord for their bountiful meal and for their new friends, Officer Pete and Kringle. The puppy in question had already eaten its fill of turkey scraps and was dozing at their feet under the table. While they ate, Pete had told stories, stories about being a cop—not the tragic ones but the heartwarming things that every cop experiences but doesn't always remember. Tabitha was enthralled, and Mrs. Cooper nodded sagely as if these were moral lessons and he was a minister expounding at the pulpit. He felt both flattered and embarrassed, but most of all he felt strangely at home.

Afterward, as he was helping Mrs. Cooper with the dishes, he happened to see Tabitha standing in the door to her bedroom with her hands over her eyes. She had turned on the light, and a pool of it had spilled out into the hall. He stood and watched her. She was peeking through the cracks in her fingers, shutting them, peeking again. Finally, she tentatively stepped inside the room. Kringle, waking from a nap, trotted down the hall and disappeared after her. Pete felt Mrs. Cooper's hand on his arm.

"Sometimes all it takes is a little time."

He nodded; he wanted to say something more, to tell her about himself, but he wasn't ready yet.

"I thank you for your hospitality, Mrs. Cooper, but I really need to go. I haven't been to sleep yet, and I work tomorrow."

Then Tabitha was standing at his elbow, Dr. Seuss book in hand. "Will you read to me?"

"Sure," he said, and he heard the crack in his voice.

DECEMBER 25, CHRISTMAS DAY: EVENING

He read for two hours in the warm and tidy little living room with both Kringle and Tabitha on his lap and Mrs. Cooper seated in her easy chair working on a pile of mending. When he finally stood up, he found his leg had gone to sleep and his voice was hoarse, but he couldn't remember when he had enjoyed himself so much. Tabitha held Kringle in her arms, snuggling the soft and pliant body as the puppy licked its own nose. She looked up at Pete and seemed to be mustering her courage. Then she asked, almost as a whisper, "Can I keep him? Please."

Pete felt a chill down his spine. He pictured his empty house without the little dog—there hadn't been life within those walls in so long, and this puppy, this strange little creature, had rescued him, it seemed, more than he had rescued it. Mrs. Cooper came to his aid.

"No, Tabitha, Kringle is Officer Pete's puppy. After the New Year we'll talk about getting you a puppy of your own."

Tabitha nodded and hung her head, touching the top of the puppy's head with her chin. Pete saw her spine stiffen as she prepared to weather yet another disappointment.

Suddenly Pete heard himself say, "You know, Tabitha, I work a lot of hours. I'm not sure I can be there for Kringle as much as he needs me to be. Maybe you would be willing to take care of him for me."

She looked up, her eyes filled with tears. "I can take good care of him for you."

When Pete walked down the sidewalk to his truck, he felt a sense of loss like acid in his intestines. He was losing his family again and going home alone. He knew that the puppy belonged with the child, and he knew that this day, this wonderful Christmas day, wouldn't happen again. It was just chance that it had happened at all. Now it was back to real life. He would go back to his empty house, and this little family would resume at exactly the point where he had found it. He knew he should be grateful for the last few days, but he was tired of being grateful for what he once had rather than for what he had now.

As he sat in his truck, letting the engine warm up, he saw Tabitha and Mrs. Cooper come out the front door, both bundled in their winter coats and carrying brown grocery sacks. He saw that Tabitha was wearing the red parka he'd given Amy for her sixth birthday. He put the truck in gear and pulled up beside them.

"Are you going to church? I can give you both a ride."

"That's all right, Pete," said Mrs. Cooper. "The bus stops right there at the corner."

"Come on, let me give you a ride."

Tabitha looked at him with her big eyes. "We're not going to the church right now, Officer Pete."

Mrs. Cooper pulled her collar up on her coat. "I made her a Christmas promise."

Tabitha nodded. "We're going to visit my daddy."

Pete was disconcerted; he thought her daddy was . . . then he realized where they were going.

"You're going out to Woodlawn?"

Tabitha nodded.

"I'm going that way myself. Hop in."

Pete drove and Mrs. Cooper held Tabitha on her lap. He reached down under the seat and made sure that his gun was pushed way back out of reach. He didn't say anything, just kept his eyes on the road, and the old woman and the little girl didn't say anything, either. He was thinking that the cheer had drained out of Christmas for all of them, but maybe he was just tired. He knew that this was not an errand he would enjoy. But he was used to steeling himself, wasn't he? This was, after all, how he had lived his life for years. He caught a glimpse of his impassive face in the glass and thought that once again he looked older.

It was very dark when they reached the cemetery, less than an hour until closing, and everyone who had visited that day and left wreaths and trees on the graves had gone. Pete realized that Mrs. Cooper and Tabitha must have intended to make this pilgrimage much earlier in the day but had chosen to spend the time with him instead.

"There," said Mrs. Cooper. "My son is buried right over there."

Pete started. For some reason he had thought of the young man with the Camels in his pocket only as Tabitha's father. Somehow it hadn't registered that he was also Mrs. Cooper's son.

He waited for them as they went over to the grave hand in hand, an old woman and her small grandchild, and he watched them as they knelt down to brush away the debris, decorated the headstone with Christmas ornaments, and lit a candle.

Pete leaned back against a denuded tree and wished he had brought his bottle of scotch. It was freezing out there and smelled vaguely moldy, and he realized how lonely a cemetery was after dark. He tried to keep focused on the slender backs of the old woman and the small child, but finally he couldn't stop himself. He started off to find the adjacent graves of his wife and daughter.

He didn't know how long he had been standing there, staring down at their names, STACY GRISWOLD, AMY GRISWOLD . . . BELOVED WIFE AND MOTHER. BELOVED DAUGHTER, but he felt rain slipping under his coat collar and running down the back of his neck. It was cold, too cold, but not cold enough to snow. He had never visited their graves, not since he stood with the other mourners and watched the two caskets lowered into the ground. He knew they weren't in there. He had seen both their bodies after the crash, and there had been so little that he could recognize. They had fled those bodies, he had thought, on impact, and their immortal souls were whole and perfect. Now, looking down, he wondered if they had been as lonely for him as he had been for them. That's when he felt a tiny hand slip into his.

"Amy?" he said, but he looked down into Tabitha's solemn eyes.

"That was your little girl's name?"

He nodded, and Tabitha opened the brown paper sack she held in her other hand and took out a tiny handmade Christmas wreath entwined with ivy. She set it between the two headstones. She looked up at Pete and took her hand away and clasped both hands in prayer.

"Dear Jesus, please thank Amy for giving me all her nice things. Please keep her soul in heaven with her mama and my daddy, too. Most of all, Jesus, keep Grandmother safe, and thank you for sending Amy's daddy to me. Amen."

Pete didn't remember the ride back to their little house on the Westside; he only remembered the warmth in the car and the swish of the truck's tires on the wet pavement. He watched them both get out of the truck. Mrs. Cooper held his hand in both of hers and kissed him on the cheek. Tabitha took off running, calling for him to wait a minute while she ran into the house.

Tabitha came back to the side of his truck with Kringle in her arms, and as he reached down to pet the puppy good-bye, she lifted him through the window.

"Bring him back on your way to work tomorrow, Officer Pete, and I'll take care of him for you."

Then she was gone, and the gleeful puppy was jumping up and down in his lap, licking his face.

Mrs. Cooper stood in the doorway and waved and called out, "See you tomorrow!" before she shut the door.

Pete looked down at Kringle and kissed the puppy on the top of its head.

"Let's go home and get to bed, boy. We've got a lot to do tomorrow." He was looking forward to it; he was looking forward to everything.